# Get Wise!™

## MASTERING Vocabulary SKILLS

### by Nathan Barber

**THOMSON**

**PETERSON'S**™

Australia • Canada • Mexico • Singapore • Spain • United Kingdom •

# THOMSON
™

## PETERSON'S

# Acknowledgments

Big thanks to Christy and Noah for putting up with my constant writing and my sense of humor (which I keep insisting they will one day learn to appreciate).

Thanks to my editor Wallie Walker Hammond for the subtle hints, "mere suggestions," advice, implicit directions, numerous rewrites, red ink everywhere, etc. (just kidding—seriously, thanks!)

Thanks to my English teachers for learning me how to write good.

A huge thanks from Christy and Noah to my editor for redirecting my sense of humor away from them!

—Nathan Barber

# Contents

OK, ready to get started? Let's begin by memorizing our first word list, which will include 25 words, all beginning with the letter *A*. When you finish, take the test on page 249.

**What? This doesn't sound like any book that I want to be in! This is supposed to be *Get Wise!* right? Or is it *Get Bored!*?**

You don't like the sound of that, Chi? What's the matter? You don't want to spend the next several weeks reading 250 pages of word lists organized alphabetically by a crusty old geezer who wears Coke-bottle glasses and has bad breath? We didn't think you did, so we reassigned that old codger to the library at the Sunnybrook Retirement Home just up the road. And with the old guy gone, it looks like things will be a bit better.

So, here's the deal. You or someone else, maybe your parents, spent some bucks on this book to help you with your vocabulary. You may be getting ready for the PSAT, SAT, an exit-level exam, or maybe vocabulary just isn't your thing. Perhaps your teacher made you get this book to help you with a course, maybe an English course or some similar course that someone made you take. Or, maybe you are one of those people who account for only a tiny fraction of a percent of the entire population of the free world who buys self-help test-prep books to read for fun on the weekends after you finish all your other homework and the extra-credit work your teacher offered. (If this isn't you, you know the type we're talking about.)

Whatever the situation, lucky you gets to work on vocab. Well, guess what? Been there and done that. But we did this routine with a boring teacher, a boring book, and alphabetical lists. We were bored. In fact, we were so bored that we would never wish that boredom on anybody else. Therefore, our goal is to help you learn some vocab and keep you interested at the same time. Don't think we can do it? Well, we can't do it alone. You have to help some. An open mind and a positive attitude would be great for starters. Would an eagerness to learn new words and a yearning to expand your educational horizons be too much to ask?

**Got the open mind and the positive `tude, but the only yearning I have so far is to go to the mall!**

Seriously, why learn new vocab anyway? Just for the test? OK, a great test score will go a long way toward getting you into the college you want to attend, but should that be the only reason to learn some new words? We don't think so. We think maybe, just maybe, an expanded word palette might actually be useful to you.

## How New Vocab Can Improve Your Life

★ You can drop a few big words on your parents and they'll think you've matured!

★ You can use some fancy words in your college interview and the admissions officer will think you're a genius!

★ You can use some impressive words the first time you meet your girlfriend's parents and they'll think, "What a nice boy."

See? Vocabulary *can* be pretty useful.

Back to the word lists for a minute. Yes, this book will use word lists (it is a vocab book, you know). Most vocabulary and language experts agree that you will learn the words best if the words are grouped in a meaningful way. Therefore, every group of words will have something in common to help you remember them better. In addition, we don't really expect you to just memorize word lists. Instead, you will be able to see the words used in sentences. Also, we'll throw some word games in the mix to keep it interesting and to make you think a little bit.

If you spend just 20 minutes every day with this book, you will have a huge advantage heading into the PSAT or SAT or any other standardized test. No matter what others will tell you, the verbal sections of these tests are vocabulary tests. Sure, they do some different things with the words, like context clues and word association. But do you think you can answer the questions if you don't know what the words mean? Nope. We don't think so, either. If you are using this as a companion text for a course, you may make improvements in your work almost immediately. Either way, just a few minutes a day with this book, and that's all you'll need to make this work.

Before we get to the actual vocab lessons, we'll do a quick rundown of prefixes, suffixes, and roots. After that, we'll jump right into the vocab. So, whenever you're ready . . .

**All right, I guess I better get started. Besides, the sooner I start, the sooner I finish, and the sooner I can get to the mall!**

# chapter 1

## A Word to the Wise

About 400 years ago, a guy named William Shakespeare (maybe you've heard of him) used to make his characters sound like they didn't really know what they were talking about. We heard that audiences loved to laugh at the morons who messed up the words and made ridiculous sentences by mistake. Then, around 1775, a guy name Sheridan wrote a play called *The Rivals*.

**Uh, according to page 3, we have 20 minutes a day with this book. Wanna get to the point?**

Ok, just bear with us for a minute. In this play, Sheridan came up with a character called Miss Malaprop. Well, Miss Malaprop constantly confused

5

*Get Wise! Mastering Vocabulary Skills*                                         *www.petersons.com*

words and used wrong and inappropriate words, which really made her look like a buffoon. OK, here's the point. People for centuries have loved to laugh at the "verbally challenged," and things are still the same today. Let's face it, don't you tune in to those cheesy shows like "Blind Date," "Elimidate," and "Rendez-View" just to see what the dumb guys or totally clueless girls will say next to embarrass themselves and their entire families? Still don't see our point? Keep reading a little further.

The SAT, PSAT, and other standardized tests are great motivators for learning vocabulary. However, it might not be such a bad idea to brush up on your vocab in order to avoid sounding like that big, lumbering football player in your history class who thought that Napoleon invented the three-flavored ice cream that your grandparents buy by the gallon. Or what about the cheerleader who asked why all the fire *distinguishers* are red? Surely you don't want to be guilty of such a "malapropism"! Don't you feel a little smarter just knowing what a malapropism is? With the help of this book, you will be infinitely less likely to commit the same kinds of verbal blunders as those malapropisms.

**Napoleon ice cream and a fire distinguisher? I would *never* make an *era* like that! Why are you laughing at me? Stop it!**

We realize you could probably just pick up this book and know exactly how to use it, but just to make sure, we figured we better give you a few tips, pointers, bits of advice, etc. (Actually, our editors thought that some of you would use the book incorrectly if we didn't include some type of directions for you! Go figure!) First, don't read the book in one sitting. As tempting as it will be to stay up all night and read this page-turner in its entirety, you will have to exercise some self-discipline and break your study sessions into smaller chunks—let's say 20 minutes per day. Next, don't write down all these words on your hands and arms. Get yourself some index cards and make flashcards. Finally, tell all your friends, teachers, their friends, and their friends' teachers' friends to buy this book because there are just too darn many verbally challenged people out there filling our ears with those awful malapropisms.

One of the best ways to figure out what a word means or what word to use in a given situation is to understand the smaller parts of words that make up those fancy, often confusing words that so many people don't know how to correctly use. The next chapter, which you are no doubt dying to get to, will give you a detailed look at the word parts, or *roots*.

**I sure hope that chapter is nowhere close to the length of that TV movie *Roots*! It took a whole week to watch that thing! Don't get me wrong, it was really good, but a week?**

# chapter 2

## Word Parts

We'll probably date ourselves here, but there once was an advertising campaign used by a fast food restaurant that centered on the phrase "Parts is parts." They meant that the chicken nuggets made by their competitors were made of chicken "parts" and not the good meat from a chicken. Remember these commercials? We were afraid you wouldn't. Anyway, you're probably wondering where this is going. Bear with us because we really do have a point. Words are kind of like the other guys' chicken nuggets— made of parts. The core of a word is called a *root* and the root is often surrounded by other parts called *prefixes* and *suffixes*. Let's take a closer, but brief, look at how word parts work:

1.  **Prefixes**—These parts attach to the beginning of a root word to alter its meaning or create a new word.

2.  **Roots**—The basic element of a word that determines its meaning. Groups of words from the same root word are called word families.

3. **Suffixes—**These parts attach to the end of a root word to change its meaning, help make it grammatically correct in context, or form a new word.

Keep in mind that a word can have a root and a prefix, a root and a suffix, a root and two prefixes, a root and two suffixes, and so on. Basically, just as with the manufacturing of chicken nuggets (if you have enough parts, you can make countless nuggets), if you have enough word parts, you can make countless words. Although there seem to be no rules about parts when making chicken nuggets, there is a rule about making words: Every word must have a root.

**Well, am I the only one who's hungry now?**

Let's take a look at a list of some of the most common word parts. We'll start with prefixes, then roots and suffixes. You should read through this list carefully. We know that we've given you only the "a" words, but that's just to get you started. There's an additional list in the Appendix at the end of the book that you should go to every now and then to get a handle on how word parts work. We sure don't expect you to sit down and memorize these lists, but you should work at trying to figure out the meanings of these word parts when you see them in vocabulary words.

## PREFIXES

| Prefix | Meaning | Example |
|---|---|---|
| a- | in, on, of, to | *abed*—in bed |
| a-, ab-, abs- | from, away | *abrade*—wear off |
| | | *absent*—away, not present |
| a-, an- | lacking, not | *asymptomatic*—showing no symptoms |
| | | *anaerobic*—able to live without air |
| ac-, ad-, af-, ag-, al-, an-, ap-, ar-, as-, at- | to, toward | *accost*—approach and speak to |
| | | *adjunct*—something added to |
| | | *aggregate*—bring together |
| ambi-, amphi- | around, both | *ambidextrous*—using both hands equally |
| | | *amphibious*—living both in water and on land |

## ROOTS

| Root | Meaning | Examples |
|---|---|---|
| acr | bitter | *acrid, acrimony* |
| act, ag | do, act, drive | *action, react, agitate* |
| acu | sharp, keen | *acute, acumen* |
| agog | leader | *pedagogue, demagogic* |
| agr | field | *agronomy, agriculture* |
| ali | other | *alias, alienate, inalienable* |
| alt | high | *altitude, contralto* |

## SUFFIXES

| Suffix | Meaning | Example |
|--------|---------|---------|
| **-able, -ble** | able, capable | *acceptable*—able to be accepted |
| **-acious, -cious** | characterized by, having the quality of | *fallacious*—having the quality of a fallacy |
| **-age** | sum, total | *mileage*—total number of miles |
| **-al** | of, like, suitable for | *theatrical*—suitable for theater |
| **-ance, -ancy** | act or state of | *disturbance*—act of disturbing |
| **-ant, -ent** | one who | *defendant*—one who defends himself or herself |
| **-ary, -ar** | having the nature of, concerning | *military*—relating to soldiers *polar*—concerning the pole |

*See Appendix on page 193 for more prefixes, roots, and suffixes.*

This probably looks more like a lot of trouble, but just remember that if you can see the word parts in vocab words, then you can figure out what the words mean. And by the way, if you can identify those chicken parts in chicken nuggets, you should probably go eat somewhere else.

# Get Wise!

Instead of matching, filling in the blank, or something else along those lines, here is your "assignment." We have given you two prefixes, two roots, and three suffixes from the previous list. In the spaces below, use them to create new words. Use your imagination and be creative.

| PREFIXES | ROOTS | SUFFIXES | WORD |
|----------|-------|----------|------|
| ab– | | | |
| | alt | | |
| | agr | | |
| an– | | | |
| | | –able | |
| | | –acious | |
| | | –ent | |

# chapter 3

## Words to Make Your Parents Think You're Wise

We've already determined that a good vocabulary will help tremendously on standardized tests and in classes at school. Now let's see how an expanded vocabulary can be useful in other places as well. Each of the vocab lessons throughout the rest of the book will focus on a group of words that has something in common. In this lesson, we'll look at some words you can drop at the dinner table or before you go out on Friday night. Be sure to read the sentences that follow so you can see how the words are used. You may even want to jot these down or commit them to memory so you can use them with your parents later. Your parents will wonder what has gotten into you! Just wait and see. And since Chi needs to put her two cents into everything, she'll give you a sample sentence or two throughout the book. Here's your first list:

**15**

*Get Wise! Mastering Vocabulary Skills*     www.petersons.com

**abstain** (noun) to refrain, to hold back. *Dad, I promise that my friends and I will **abstain** from any mischief tonight if we can borrow your car.*

**ambiguous** (adjective) having two or more possible meanings, unclear. *Mom, why is Dad being **ambiguous** about the way your meatloaf tastes?*

**amiable** (adjective) likable, friendly. *I think you'll like my date for tonight; he is very **amiable**.*

**amicable (adjective) likable, agreeable.**

Mom, my friends said that you and Dad are both very **amicable**. May I have all twelve of them over for dinner?

**clandestine** (adjective) secret, surreptitious. *I can assure you both that I will participate in no **clandestine** activities while you are out of town.*

**demure** (adjective) modest or shy. *Dad, be nice to my date tonight because he is rather **demure** and I don't want you to freak him out like you did with the last guy.*

**emulate** (verb) to imitate or copy. *I always try to **emulate** the safe manner in which you drive. May I have the keys now?*

**maturation** (noun) the process of becoming fully grown or developed. *Mom, Dad, you should know that your strict discipline has contributed to my **maturation**. What do you say we extend my curfew by 2 hours?*

**meticulous** (adjective) very careful with details. *I will be very **meticulous** when I clean my room this weekend.*

**therapeutic** (adjective) curing or helping to cure. *You know what? The first week of my grounding has been very **therapeutic**. Can we forget about the second week?*

**It might be a good idea to make flashcards of these words so you can review them later. Also, keeping flashcards in your pocket is a good way to convince your parents that you are going to study at your friend's house!**

Well, what do you think? See anything you can use? Good words, huh? OK, spend a few minutes reviewing the words, then do the following exercise and we'll see if you are any wiser.

# Get Wise!

Fill in the blank with the correct word from the list above.

1. His name should be Messy Marvin because he is the least _____ person I know.

2. The directions were so _____ that I had no idea how to answer the test questions.

3. You should be flattered that your little sister tries to _____ your actions.

4. That new teacher is neither _____ nor _____; in fact, he is downright rude!

5. I don't think anyone has ever used the word _____ to describe Madonna.

6. A hammock, a Walkman, and a CD burned with my favorite bands can be very _____.

**7.** I wonder how many _____ operations our military conducted during the Cold War.

**8.** I hope my puppy will stop chewing up my shoes when he reaches _____.

**9.** The coach asked the cheerleaders to _____ from cheering when the other team scored.

## How Wise?

1. meticulous; 2. ambiguous; 3. emulate; 4. amiable; amicable; 5. demure; 6. therapeutic; 7. clandestine; 8. maturation; 9. abstain

# Words to Make Your Teachers Think You're Wise

Let's face it. You spend as much, if not more, time in school than anywhere else and your teachers are a huge part of your life. Also, you probably are going to need some of your teachers to write college recommendations for you at some point in the future. Why not impress your teachers (not just your English teacher) with an amazing vocabulary?

Throw around some of these words in class, and you can be the teacher's pet—always a good thing!

19

**absolve** (verb) to free from guilt, to exonerate. *I feel sure the videotape of the locker room will* **absolve** *him of the alleged theft.*

**anarchy** (noun) absence of law and order. *Please don't go to another teachers' conference;* **anarchy** *breaks out every time you leave a substitute with us.*

**bourgeois (adjective) middle class or reflecting middle-class values.**

The new girl with green, spiked hair is pretty cool, but she sure did shock our **bourgeois** administration.

**conundrum** (noun) a riddle, puzzle, or problem. *The way that several teachers always seem to give tests on the same day is a* **conundrum** *that we students have yet to understand.*

**critique** (noun or verb) a critical evaluation or to give a critical evaluation. *Since you are an expert, would you please read my research paper and give me a* **critique** *of my writing style?*

**diligent** (adjective) working hard and steadily. *I promise I will be* **diligent** *in my efforts to get to class on time this semester.*

**emend** (verb) to correct or improve. *I value your expert opinion, so I decided to* **emend** *my research paper as you suggested in your critique.*

**exemplary** (adjective) worthy to serve as a model. *I should nominate you for "Teacher of the Year" for your* **exemplary** *classroom manner.*

**fallacy** (noun) an error in fact or logic. *There is a* **fallacy** *in your reasoning if you believe all students love geometry.*

**transmute** (verb) to change in form or substance. *The coach somehow was able to* **transmute** *that couch potato into an All-State football player.*

If you do become the teacher's pet because of your new and improved vocab, remember to milk it for all its worth!

Did you recognize some of these words? Most of these words? Good. Take a few minutes to review them and then do the following exercise to see if you remember them all.

# Get Wise!

Fill in the blank with the correct word from the list on page 20.

**1.** The students have signed a petition requesting that the school board _____ the current dress code and allow miniskirts and short shorts.

**2.** I pleaded with the cop to _____ me of my traffic violation, but she gave me a ticket anyway.

**3.** He is so talented. He always knows how to _____ a piece of clay into a beautiful sculpture of a supermodel.

**4.** If she is elected as the class president, there will be _____ in the senior class because she's only popular with her handful of friends.

**5.** We had to be _____, but we finally were able to get the locker open and get the gum unstuck from the lock.

**6.** She was so confused about the things she heard in the halls that virtually everything she repeated was a _____.

**7.** The guys who drive expensive cars are usually pretty rich, but the rest of us are basically just _____.

**8.** You can be sure it was not _____ behavior that landed those two in detention!

**9.** We have quite a _____ on our hands. It seems that someone moved a Volkswagen onto the 50-yard line of the football field and we have no idea who did it!

**10.** Don't you just want to scream when teachers _____ every little thing on your paper and use up three red pens in the process?

## How Wise?

1. emend; 2. absolve; 3. transmute; 4. anarchy; 5. diligent; 6. fallacy; 7. bourgeois; 8. exemplary; 9. conundrum; 10. critique

# Words to Make Your Boss Think You're Wise

Do you have a job yet? If you do, you know how important it is to impress your boss and make your boss believe you know what you're doing there. And do you remember trying to impress the person who interviewed you for the job? Of course you do.

If you don't have a job yet, you will before you know it. When you interview for that first job, you'll want to make a good impression on the interviewer (believe us, you will). Here's how you do it:

★ **Be confident.**

★ **Look that interviewer in the eye.**

★ **Use good vocabulary.**

Believe it or not, employers actually look for things like a good vocabulary because that shows intelligence. Really, it does. Our next list gives you those words that will impress your boss or your interviewer. Definitely keep these in mind when you get that job. Your parents will be extremely impressed (isn't that the point?), and all of that extra money will come in handy.

**adaptable** (adjective) able to be changed to be suitable for a new purpose. *I think you will find that I'm very* **adaptable** *and I can handle any new responsibilities you have for me.*

**astute (adjective) observant and attentive, intelligent, shrewd.**

Uh, I didn't catch that last question. Could you please repeat it? Oh, yes, I would consider myself very **astute**.

**collaborate** (verb) to work together. *Sir, I think you are a genius. I would love the opportunity to* **collaborate** *with you on this project.*

**competent** (adjective) having the skill and knowledge needed for a particular task; capable. *I believe I am the most qualified and* **competent** *applicant for this job. What? I was the only applicant?*

**mediocrity** (noun) the state of being middling or poor in quality. *I can assure you that* **mediocrity** *is not even in my vocabulary!*

**perceptive** (adjective) quick to notice, observant. *I think you will find that I am very* **perceptive** *and I pay close attention to details.*

**reputable** (adjective) having a good reputation. *I would consider myself fortunate to have the opportunity to work with a firm as* **reputable** *as yours.*

**scrupulous** (adjective) acting with extreme care. *No matter how great or small the task that I am assigned, I assure you I will be most* **scrupulous** *as I perform the task.*

**transient** (adjective) passing quickly. *I know you don't like to hire transient workers, so I have decided to stay in the area for at least two years.*

**utilitarian** (adjective) purely of practical benefit. *I think you will find that I am a no-nonsense, utilitarian person who can do without excesses and luxuries.*

**Remember those flashcards I mentioned earlier? Well, I hope they're not *still* in your pocket! You won't be impressing anybody if you've got cards sticking out of your clothes!**

Those are some good words that should come in pretty handy. Just remember that if you get a job because of vocab that you learned from this book, you owe us a cut of your first three months' salary! Didn't you read the fine print on the title page? Too late now!

# Get Wise!

Let's try some opposites. Fill in each blank with one of the words you just learned that means the opposite of the word(s) next to the blank.

1. _____ inept, incapable

2. _____ permanent

3. _____ inattentive, dimwitted

4. _____ inflexible

5. _____ act independently

6. _____ frivolous, impractical

7. _____ dishonest, untrustworthy

8. _____ superiority, excellence

9. _____ unaware

10. _____ imprecise

# How Wise?

1. competent; 2. transient; 3. astute; 4. adaptable; 5. collaborate; 6. utilitarian; 7. reputable; 8. mediocrity; 9. perceptive; 10. scrupulous

# Words to Make Your Boss Think You're <u>Not</u> Very Wise

In the previous chapter, we asked if you have a job. Now the question is, "Do you want to *keep* your job?" The words in this chapter probably won't really cost you your job, but they'll certainly make your boss look at you a second time. Your boss will think you have a nice vocabulary, but these aren't exactly the best words to throw around at the office:

Hey, if you just want to have a little fun with your boss or make your supervisor squirm a little, then go ahead and try these at work.

**27**

*Get Wise! Mastering Vocabulary Skills*                     www.petersons.com

**dawdle** (verb) to procrastinate, dally, or idle. *The fact that I often **dawdle** when it comes to my work shouldn't bother you; I work best under pressure.*

**embezzle** (verb) to steal or misappropriate funds or assets. *How upset would you be if a certain employee were to **embezzle** a few dollars here and a few dollars there? No reason, just curious.*

**fugitive** (noun) someone trying to escape. May *I still work here even if I become a **fugitive**? I can keep a secret if you can.*

**lethargic (adjective) lacking energy; sluggish.**

Is there any chance I could start work at 11:00 instead of 8:00? I tend to be rather **lethargic** in the morning.

**malinger** (verb) to pretend incapacity or illness to avoid a duty or work. *Is there any way for you to know if an employee is **malingering** instead of actually being sick?*

**novice** (noun) beginner. *I guess I should have mentioned that I was a **novice** before you let me operate the heavy machinery by myself.*

**sycophant** (noun) flatterer. *I heard that the guy in the next cubicle accused me of being a **sycophant**. Sir, surely someone with your sage-like wisdom and superior intelligence knows that isn't true.*

**truant** (adjective) absent without permission. *I wasn't **truant** yesterday. I was just really tired from the weekend, so I caught up on my sleep. Did I miss anything important?*

**unkempt** (adjective) messy or untidy. *Is there anything in my contract prohibiting me from coming to work **unkempt** and disheveled?*

**volatile** (adjective) quickly changing; fleeting, transitory; prone to violence. *No, thanks. If I have that fifth cup of coffee, I may become **volatile**; caffeine makes me a little crazy sometimes.*

Gee, these sentences sure did remind me of that movie *Office Space.* Did you see it? Wasn't it great? And you thought smart people only watch TLC and CSPAN!

We sure hope you can see how either your boss or a prospective employer might not like to hear you bringing these words to a conversation. You don't? Well, can't say we didn't warn you.

# Get Wise!

For each of the following word groups, circle the one word that does *not* belong.

**1.** pilfer      embezzle      return      thieve

**2.** malinger      lounge      loaf      exert

**3.** explosive      eruptive      volatile      pacific

**4.** lethargic      torpid      energetic      slumberous

**5.** rookie      veteran      novice      neophyte

**6.** escapee      fugitive      prisoner      derelict

**7.** delay      dally      dawdle      hasten

**8.** toady      sycophant      oracle      yes-man

**9.** disorderly      unclean      unkempt      immaculate

**10.** present      truant      missing      awol

# How Wise?

1. return; 2. exert; 3. pacific; 4. energetic; 5. veteran; 6. prisoner; 7. hasten; 8. oracle; 9. immaculate; 10. present

# chapter 7

## Words to Make Your Friends Think You're Wiser Than They

OK, make sure you don't tell anybody this chapter is in here. Other than the people at the printer, you're the only other person who knows this chapter made its way into the book. We worked a deal with the folks at the printer to add this chapter on the "down low" (or the Q.T., if that's where you're from). The words in this chapter are all words you can use with your friends. See if they have any idea what you're talking about! *You* sound smart, *they* may look, well, not so smart, and you get your point across.

You can also use these on your little brother or sister. Do you really think your parents are going to complain about your

**31**

*Get Wise! Mastering Vocabulary Skills*                    *www.petersons.com*

**hackneyed (adjective) without originality, trite.**

Do you have an original thought in that cavernous head of yours? Everything that comes out of your mouth sounds **hackneyed**.

**incorrigible** (adjective) impossible to manage or reform. *As many times as you've been in trouble and you still act that way? You're simply **incorrigible**!*

**malediction** (noun) curse. *If only I could strike you with a **malediction** and you'd just disappear!*

**ostentatious** (adjective) overly showy, pretentious. *The outfits you wear certainly qualify you for this year's "Most **Ostentatious**" award.*

**pariah** (noun) outcast. *You think you're popular, but everyone else considers you a **pariah**.*

**pugnacious** (adjective) combative, bellicose, truculent; ready to fight. *With that **pugnacious** attitude of yours, it's a wonder no one has punched you in the nose!*

**querulous** (adjective) complaining, whining. *Must you be **querulous** every time you don't get your way? You're acting like a big baby.*

**tedium** (noun) boredom. *Listening to your stories fills me with a **tedium** that is really hard to describe.*

**treacherous** (adjective) untrustworthy or disloyal; dangerous or unreliable. *No one tells you the latest scoop because you have proven that you are simply the most **treacherous** person in the tenth grade.*

**trite** (adjective) boring because of over-familiarity. *That story is so **trite** that it makes me sleepy. You know I've heard that one fifty times.*

Hey, you've got to admit that these words are better than those four-letter words you *can't* use in front of parents and teachers. With these words, you can sound smart *and* you can say them anywhere! What a deal!

Can't you just see those confused looks on your friends' faces while they try to figure out what the heck you're talking about?

# Get Wise!

Match the vocabulary word with its synonym.

| | | | | |
|---|---|---|---|---|
| 1. | _____ hackneyed | | **A.** untrustworthy |
| 2. | _____ incorrigible | | **B.** pompous |
| 3. | _____ malediction | | **C.** discontented |
| 4. | _____ ostentatious | | **D.** uncontrollable |
| 5. | _____ pariah | | **E.** damnation |
| 6. | _____ pugnacious | | **F.** commonplace |
| 7. | _____ querulous | | **G.** insipid |
| 8. | _____ tedium | | **H.** bum |
| 9. | _____ treacherous | | **I.** antagonistic |
| 10. | _____ trite | | **J.** doldrums |

# How Wise?

1. G; 2. D; 3. E; 4. B; 5. H; 6. I; 7. C; 8. J; 9. A; 10. F

## Puzzle 1

Complete the following puzzle using the words you just learned in this chapter. Puzzle solutions are in the back of the book.

**Across**

8. change

11. boring

14. beginner

15. fake illness

16. runaway

18. whining

20. no government

**Down**

1. puzzle

2. untidy

3. absent

4. quickly changing

5. trustworthy

6. observant

7. careful

9. exonerate

10. boredom

12. outcast

13. modest

17. error

19. correct

# Wise or Not So Wise—Ways to Improve a Research Paper

You're probably thinking that, from the title of this chapter, these words will be ones you can use in your research paper to get that instant "A". Well, that isn't exactly what we're going for here. These words are great vocab words for you to know, but about the research paper . . . We know your teachers set certain limits for your papers, either word limits or page limits. More often than not, these limits are minimum limits. Well, don't you feel bad for these teachers who have to read through as many as hundreds of these so-called research papers? The words we're giving you can help you help your teachers avoid reading those long, "I couldn't stop writing" assignments. And you'll finish your papers faster than ever before! Study the list and you'll see what we mean.

35

*Get Wise! Mastering Vocabulary Skills*  www.petersons.com

**abbreviate** (verb) to make briefer, to shorten. *Mr. Jones, so you don't have to read so many pages, I decided to* **abbreviate** *every proper name, title, and practically every other word that was longer than six letters. Enjoy!*

**abridge** (verb) to shorten, to reduce. *Mrs. Montanez, my original paper was fourteen pages long. I didn't want you to spend all weekend grading, so I decided to* **abridge** *my paper for you and the whole thing is now two pages!*

**alacrity** (noun) promptness, speed. *Ms. McCarron, I know you must get tired of reading so many papers, so I abridged my paper so you could read it with greater* **alacrity**.

**belated** (adjective) delayed past the proper time. *Mrs. Rosenberg, I apologize for the* **belated** *paper, but I just didn't think it was good enough to turn in on the due date. Those extra three weeks I spent on it, though, have given me enough time to get it just right!*

**bereft (adjective) lacking or deprived of something.**

Mr. Barton, you said my rough draft was **bereft** of something that could make my paper stand out. So I printed the research paper on orange stationery and added about ten pictures.

**curtail** (verb) to shorten. *Right in the middle of my writing, I thought about all those dreadful papers you would have to grade, Mr. Jordan, so I decided to* **curtail** *my efforts and end the paper ahead of schedule for you.*

**discredit** (verb) to cause disbelief in the accuracy of some statement or the reliability of a person. *My paper has a revolutionary new thesis. I didn't want to* **discredit** *all those encyclopedias and scholarly journals, Mr. Hall, so I just left out all those citations you wanted.*

**divulge** (verb) to reveal. *Mrs. Hollingsworth, because I used Top Secret government documents for my research, I left out all the citations because it might endanger me if I* **divulge** *my sources.*

**frivolity** (noun) lack of seriousness; levity. *Mr. Livingstone, "Social and Economic Causes of the French Revolution" seemed like such a serious and boring subject, so I changed the assignment a little. To add a little* **frivolity**, *I changed the title to "Social and Economic Causes of the Success of "The Jerry Springer Show."*

**superficial** (adjective) on the surface only; without depth or substance. *Mr. Cartwright, I found that "The Psyche of Albert Einstein" is far too deep for me to cover in a five-page paper. Therefore, I did a more* **superficial** *look at him called, "What's Up with Einstein's Hair?"*

**Hey! I thought this was a vocab book, not a writing skills book! I should get my money back. Oh, my bad...**

By the way, on your next research paper, don't use this book as a reference and don't take our advice on writing papers. (Maybe you should check out *Get Wise! Mastering Writing Skills*.) OK? Just take the vocab and spice things up a little with your new word power.

## Get Wise!

Circle the word that does <u>not</u> belong in each word group.

1. abbreviate    shorten    extend    contract

2. digest    abridge    compress    increase

3. sloth    quickness    alacrity    promptness

4. tardy    belated    timely    overdue

5. bereft    without    full    lacking

6. trim    curtail    reduce    lengthen

7. prove    discredit    disprove    tarnish

8. confess    hide    divulge    reveal

9. whimsicality    frivolity    seriousness    capriciousness

10. cursory    in-depth    shallow    superficial

## How Wise?

1. extend; 2. increase; 3. sloth; 4. timely; 5. full; 6. lengthen; 7. prove; 8. hide; 9. seriousness; 10. in-depth

# A Wise Person Has Many Friends

OK, now, doesn't that sound like something Confucius would say? Who's Confucius? We guess you were absent that day in World History. Anyway, back to the friends. As we all know, friends are probably the most important things you will acquire in the next several years. At this point in your life, your friends may very well be the most important part of your life. Heck, they *are* the most important. (Have your parents and teachers figured that out yet?) Since your friends are such a huge part of your life, shouldn't you know some words to help describe your relationship with your friends? Of course you should, and here they are:

**I tried to convince them to include words in this section like *homeys*, *chill,* and *down with that,* but they had no idea what I was talking about. Sorry.**

**camaraderie** (noun) a spirit of friendship. *My boys and I have a sense of camaraderie that nobody, not even a girl, can break.*

**cohesive** (adjective) sticking together, unified. *That group of girls is so cohesive that they'll stand by each other through anything.*

**confidant (noun) someone entrusted with another's secret.**

A true friend is also a **confidant** whom I can trust with any secrets or gossip.

**discreet** (adjective) showing good judgment in speech and behavior. *Real friends are **discreet** and careful about how they talk about their friends.*

**fraternize** (verb) to associate with on friendly terms. ***Fraternizing*** *with my friends at the lake on the weekends is one of my favorite things to do.*

**nurture** (verb) to nourish or help grow. *A good circle of friends will help to **nurture** and develop social skills.*

**ostracize** (verb) to exclude from a group. *Anyone who would **ostracize** someone else probably isn't a very good friend.*

**polarize** (adjective) to separate into opposing groups or forces. *Nothing can **polarize** two friends like a member of the opposite sex.*

**reconcile** (verb) to make consistent or harmonious. *When two friends have a disagreement, it is very important for them to **reconcile** their differences as soon as possible.*

**unstinting** (adjective) giving freely and generously. *The best friends are* **unstinting** *with their time and never act jealous or envious.*

**Isn't it funny how your friends can be so great one minute and then absolutely turn against you the next? I know these two girls who . . . Oh, that's right, it's supposed to be a secret. Can't tell you. Sorry `bout that.**

Next time you hang with your friends, try using some of these words on them. They'll wonder who you are and what you did with their real friend!

# Get Wise!

Fill in the blank with the appropriate word.

1. We worked hard to _____ our relationship with the jocks, but all they wanted to do was pump iron.

2. If you want everyone in school to know something, just tell that girl who is never _____ about anything.

3. She is infamous for her _____ efforts to give free fashion advice.

4. Preseason football training in grueling conditions with your friends really helps build _____ among players.

**5.** The preps were quick to _____ him for wearing spring colors after Labor Day.

**6.** It was quite touching to see the students in the computer club _____ after the big "PC versus MAC" debate in the lab.

**7.** The homecoming queen election did more to _____ the student body than did the debate over who got the best spaces in the parking lot.

**8.** The basketball team became an incredibly _____ unit after the coach announced that this would be his last season.

**9.** Our cheerleaders like to _____ with the players more than they like to cheer for the team.

**10.** He is no longer my _____ because he told practically everyone that I have a crush on Carson Daly.

## How Wise?

1. nurture; 2. discreet; 3. unstinting; 4. camaraderie; 5. ostracize; 6. reconcile; 7. polarize; 8. cohesive; 9. fraternize; 10. confidant

# chapter 10

# You're Wiser Than Most if You Know These Words

Let's face it. Even if you didn't know the actual definitions for most of the words we've covered so far, you've probably at least seen or heard them before. That's a good thing. If you are saying to yourself right now, "I knew *all* of the words," then you're just a big showoff. Well, there are quite a few words that exist somewhere out there in another universe that only occasionally appear in our world.

And when those words do appear in our world, they only show up on tests!

*Get Wise! Mastering Vocabulary Skills*                      www.petersons.com

These are words that your English teacher doesn't even use when she's trying to confuse that kid in the back row. These are just the kind of words that standardized test makers love to throw in the mix just to make you squirm. The good news for you is that you don't have to worry. We've got them covered for you. Let's take a look:

**No way you knew all of them! I'm a genius, and *I* didn't even know them all.**

**carping** (adjective) unfairly or excessively critical. *The **carping**, hugely unpopular English teacher always empties his red pen on the papers that his classes submit to him.*

**cloying** (adjective) overly sweet or sentimental. *She liked him. However, his **cloying** personality became overwhelming when he refused to wash his cheek where she kissed him.*

**connubial** (adjective) related to marriage. *The **connubial** responsibilities that come with a household to manage seem to scare many guys away from the altar.*

**enervate** (verb) to reduce the energy or strength of someone or something. *Those geometry assignments tend to **enervate** me so much that I sometimes sleep during physics.*

**interlocutor** (noun) someone taking part in a dialogue or conversation. *When the debate over the homecoming float began, there were two **interlocutors**. Within 30 minutes, though, 300 people in the cafeteria were shouting at the top of their lungs.*

**nadir** (noun) lowest point. *The **nadir** of the season for the basketball team was when they finished the game with more fouls than points.*

**obdurate** (adjective) unwilling to change; stubborn and inflexible. *The principal was absolutely **obdurate** with the punishment he handed down for riding the skateboard in the hallway.*

**penurious** (adjective) extremely frugal. *The algebra teacher was so **penurious** that he only bought items on sale for 75 percent off or more. As a result, much of his wardrobe was brown, either too large or too small, and always out of season.*

**raconteur** (noun) a skilled storyteller. *Noah, an incredible **raconteur**, is able to explain his way out of every predicament.*

**shibboleth** (noun) pet phrase, favorite saying, or slogan.

You know you might need to get a life if you use the **shibboleth** "Golly gee willikers" on a regular basis.

Once you get the hang of these words, you should use a few of them in front of that older sister who always thinks you don't know much. We can almost guarantee that she'll act like she knows what you are saying and then, as soon as you leave the room, she'll race for the dictionary to make sure you didn't just insult her. Try it. It'll be great!

# Get Wise!

Match the vocabulary word with its synonym.

1. _____ carping

2. _____ cloying

3. _____ enervate

4. _____ obdurate

5. _____ connubial

6. _____ interlocutor

7. _____ nadir

8. _____ penurious

9. _____ shibboleth

10. _____ raconteur

A. miserly

B. faultfinding

C. maudlin

D. marital

E. bard

F. bottom

G. motto

H. speaker

I. weaken

J. hard-headed

# How Wise?

1. B; 2. C; 3. I; 4. J; 5. D; 6. H; 7. F; 8. A; 9. G; 10. E

# Wise Words for Talk-Show Guests

A few years ago, the hottest thing on TV was the talk show. Jerry, Rikki, Sally, Jenny, Oprah, Montel, Maury, and the list goes on. The talk-show rage has died down some now, but some of those cable channels are still filled with talk-show wannabes who are hoping to cash in on the success of those original talk shows. The problem is that they are running out of scenarios. Here's the question: Were all the guests on those shows real, or were they just actors who couldn't get work elsewhere? There were so many episodes of those shows and so many weirdos on the shows, that surely every person in America would know at least one person who actually appeared on one of those things. Problem is, we don't. Do you? At any rate, here are some words that were made for talk-show guests.

**47**

*Get Wise! Mastering Vocabulary Skills*     *www.petersons.com*

**I've got a great idea for another book. We could call it *Talk Show Vocab: What the Heck Are They Saying, and Why Do We Care?***

**acrimonious** (adjective) biting, harsh, caustic. *No matter the topic of the show, talk-show guests always end up hitting each other and screaming* **acrimonious** *insults at one another.*

**audacious** (adjective) bold, daring, adventurous. *A person must really have to be* **audacious** *to appear on national TV and explain that he or she is not an honest person.*

**circumlocution** (noun) speaking in a roundabout way; wordiness. *People on talk shows always try to sound more intelligent than they really are and ultimately just spout off one* **circumlocution** *after another.*

**conformity** (noun) agreement with or adherence to custom or rule. *If a producer detects any hint of* **conformity** *in a potential talk-show guest, the potential guest is given no further consideration.*

**criterion (noun) a standard of measurement or judgment.**

The **criterion** for appearing on a talk show includes having at least one bizarre family member, nowhere else to be, or a mullet.

**destitute** (adjective) very poor. *Surely some of the people on talk shows were just* **destitute** *actors willing to do anything for a few bucks and a trip to New York.*

**ingenious** (adjective) showing cleverness and originality. *You must admit it was an* **ingenious** *idea to put the dregs of society on national TV to hash out their problems and insult each other.*

**prolific** (adjective) producing many offspring or creations. *Unfortunately, some of the most bizarre people on the talk shows also became* **prolific** *authors.*

**rationale** (noun) an underlying reason or explanation. *Surely there is some* **rationale** *behind the unusually strange behavior of the people on the talk shows, but it may take an expert in the field of abnormal psychology.*

**spurious** (adjective) false, fake. *Talk-show guests claim their stories are true, but most likely, their tales are* **spurious**.

**Are there any nitwits or simpletons left in America who haven't been on a talk show? Next time you're in class, look around. I bet you'll see a few who might be talk-show material.**

As you read through those words, did you have any Springer flashbacks or revisit any favorite Montel moments? It was like a walk down repressed memory lane for us.

# Get Wise!

For each of the following word groups, circle the one word that does <u>not</u> belong.

| | | | | |
|---|---|---|---|---|
| **1.** | acrimonious | caustic | sweet | sarcastic |
| **2.** | timid | audacious | bold | dauntless |
| **3.** | verbosity | brevity | tautology | circumlocution |
| **4.** | congruity | homogeneity | conformity | dissension |
| **5.** | standard | criterion | measure | abnormality |
| **6.** | poverty-stricken | destitute | rich | impoverished |
| **7.** | brilliant | adroit | ingenious | dimwitted |
| **8.** | fruitful | sterile | fertile | prolific |
| **9.** | thinking | rationale | guess | reasoning |
| **10.** | spurious | bogus | fake | veritable |

# How Wise?

1. sweet; 2. timid; 3. brevity; 4. dissension; 5. abnormality; 6. rich; 7. dimwitted; 8. sterile; 9. guess; 10. veritable

# chapter 12

# Gimme a W, Gimme an H, Gimme a Y, Gimme an S!

OK, you know where this is going. Now, don't get offended yet. We're not going to stereotype all cheerleaders, just the stereotypical ones. We know there are cheerleaders out there who make straight As, who are really nice, who are not vain, and who actually use their heads for something besides a ribbon holder. But then there are the others. Yea, you know who we're talking about. You know, the ones who yell D-E-F-E-N-S-E as their team is racing toward the endzone with football in hand. Hey, we're not making this up and you know it.

**57**

*Get Wise! Mastering Vocabulary Skills*          *www.petersons.com*

OK, now gimme a V, gimme an O, gimme a C, gimme an A, gimme a hint because I forgot the next letter.

**aesthetic** (adjective) relating to art or beauty. *Although many people think cheerleaders serve no practical or strategic purpose at games, few people question their **aesthetic** value.*

**euphoric** (adjective) a feeling of extreme happiness. *Do cheerleaders go to a special training camp to learn how to walk around and look **euphoric** all the time?*

**exuberance** (noun) a state of wild joy and enthusiasm. *Is it my imagination, or are cheerleaders often stricken with chronic **exuberance**?*

**frenetic** (adjective) chaotic, frantic. *It's amazing how cheerleaders can maintain such a **frenetic** level of physical activity during a game, but the athletes often appear to be in a vegetative state.*

**gullible** (adjective) easily fooled.

If you have a tall tale to tell, find a **gullible** cheerleader because she'll believe anything you tell her.

**idolatry** (noun) the worship of a person, thing, or institution as a god. *The computer geeks surely are guilty of **idolatry** considering the incredible Web site they created to venerate the cheerleading squad.*

**inarticulate** (adjective) unable to speak or express oneself clearly and understandably. *She sure does talk a lot for someone so **inarticulate**.*

**narcissistic** (adjective) showing excessive love for oneself. *Do some cheerleaders primp because they are **narcissistic**, or are they just participating in community beautification programs?*

**pretentious** (adjective) claiming excessive value or importance. *Maybe he wouldn't get picked on so much if he weren't so* **pretentious**.

**reprehensible** (adjective) deserving criticism or censure. *Cheerleader bashing is absolutely* **reprehensible** *behavior.*

Now, if you aren't a cheerleader, you may think that cheerleaders who read this chapter will have their feelings hurt. Let us not forget two things: first, this was all in fun, and second, cheerleaders are terminally happy so this chapter will have zero effect on them anyway.

Truth be known, we think cheerleaders are great. We fully support cheerleaders and what they try to accomplish. Remember, without cheerleaders, school environments would be less happy. Just think of how much less laughter there would be without them!

Relax! We're just playing!!

The opinions previously expressed do not reflect those of the publisher . . .They made me say that!

# Get Wise!

Fill in each blank with the appropriate vocabulary word.

**1.** The basketball game maintained a _____ pace, and both teams scored in triple digits.

**2.** Guys who are conceited and have no reason to be are just too _____ for me.

**3.** Why did they get an _____ guy to be the commencement speaker for graduation this year?

**4.** She's so _____ that I convinced her I once worked for the British spy organization with James Bond.

**5.** The _____ value of the art far outweighs its monetary value.

**6.** Their religion prohibits _____, lying, and stealing.

**7.** The chess team was filled with _____ when it won the big chess tournament.

**8.** The politician's behavior was so _____ that the constituents demanded his resignation.

**9.** She was _____ when she learned that the popular singer was out of rehab and back on the tour.

**10.** Pausing in front of every mirror is the epitome of _____ behavior.

## How Wise?

1. frenetic; 2. pretentious; 3. inarticulate; 4. gullible; 5. aesthetic; 6. idolatry; 7. exuberance; 8. reprehensible; 9. euphoric; 10. narcissistic

---

## Puzzle 2

Complete the following puzzle using the words you just learned in this chapter. Puzzle solutions are in the back of the book.

**Across**

3. standard

5. storyteller

8. deprived of

13. reveal

14. harsh

15. unified

16. shorten

17. expose as false

**Down**

1. friendship

2. exclude

3. sentimental

4. bold

6. stubborn

7. frugal

9. critical

10. conceit

11. fake

12. overthrow

13. poor

18. lowest point

# With These Words, You Could Play a Wise Doctor on TV

Have you seen that commercial where the old, out-of-work actor advertises some product by saying, "I'm not a doctor, but I do play one on TV"? Well, these vocab words may not launch an acting career that will land you on one of those infomercials, but they may make you sound a little like a neurosurgeon. Well, OK, maybe a pre-med student. Let's look at the list of words:

**alleviate** (verb) to make lighter or more bearable. *I always light a few smelly candles to help* **alleviate** *any stress I feel before my finals.*

**antiseptic** (adjective) fighting infection; extremely clean. *My mom is such an* **antiseptic** *freak that she sanitizes every inch of the house three times during the week and once on the weekend.*

**57**

*Get Wise! Mastering Vocabulary Skills*                    www.petersons.com

**discrepancy** (noun) a difference or variance between two or more things. *Because of the **discrepancy** between the two doctors' opinions about my mental state, I'm going to a third doctor.*

**emollient** (noun) something that softens or soothes. *The doctor prescribed a very expensive **emollient** for my dry, itchy, scaly rash.*

**inoculate** (verb) to prevent a disease by infusing with a disease-causing organism. *It is important to get **inoculated** before you visit some countries so you don't catch some bizarre disease.*

**pathology** (noun) disease or the study of disease; extreme abnormality. *Hey, your mom left a message at the school office. She said that the **pathology** lab called and it's going to need another sample in order to determine whether or not you are contagious.*

**purify** (verb) to make pure, clean, or perfect. *My mom, the clean freak, also has a number of contraptions that she uses to **purify** the air in the house.*

**recuperate** (verb) to regain health after an illness. *It took me six weeks to **recuperate** from my strained big toe. Don't laugh, it was a serious injury.*

**responsive** (adjective) reacting quickly and appropriately. *His disease was so **responsive** to his medication that he perked up much sooner than his doctors anticipated.*

**secrete** (verb) to emit; to hide.

The chemistry experiment began to **secrete** a disgusting substance, and the entire class lost its lunch.

**If you feel like you don't understand any of these words, then take two and call me in the morning. Two what? Beats me, but that's what those doctors always say on TV.**

If you make frequent trips to the doctor's office, you've probably heard these words. Come to think of it, you've probably heard these on "ER" or some other TV show. So you've heard them before, but did you know what they meant before today? Do you know what they mean now?

# Get Wise!

Match the vocabulary word with its synonym.

| | | |
|---|---|---|
| 1. _____ | alleviate | A. ooze |
| 2. _____ | antiseptic | B. disease research |
| 3. _____ | discrepancy | C. recover |
| 4. _____ | emollient | D. difference |
| 5. _____ | inoculate | E. rid |
| 6. _____ | pathology | F. cleanse |
| 7. _____ | purify | G. agreeable |
| 8. _____ | recuperate | H. sterile |
| 9. _____ | responsive | I. vaccinate |
| 10. _____ | secrete | J. lotion |

# How Wise?

1. E; 2. H; 3. D; 4. J; 5. I; 6. B; 7. F; 8. C; 9. G; 10. A

# chapter 14

# It Would Be Wise to Watch Your Ps and Qs, Part 1

Let's change things a little and put a different spin on a couple of these chapters. All of the words in this chapter will have something in common, but the chapter won't have a theme. All of the words in this chapter start with the letter *P*, then the next chapter will have ten words that all start with *Q*. So you think this is a silly way to organize a chapter? We think it's a great idea. Still don't think so? Try a little challenge. You have ten seconds to think of ten words . . . no, let's make it easier . . . seven words . . . with more than one syllable that start with the letter *P*. Go!

**One** . . .

**Two** . . .

**64**

*Get Wise! Mastering Vocabulary Skills*  *www.petersons.com*

Three . . .

Four . . .

Five . . .

Six . . .

Seven . . .

Eight . . . .

Nine . . .

Ten . . .

Couldn't do it, could you? We didn't think so. The next time someone asks you to name seven words that start with *P*, you'll be able to give them at least ten. And here they are:

**paroxysm** (noun) a fit or tantrum. *My grandfather said my dad once threw a conniption fit. Is that old folks' language for a* **paroxysm***?*

**perdition** (noun) damnation, destruction. *That old math teacher used to threaten kids with* **perdition** *if they were late for class.*

**perfunctory** (adjective) unenthusiastic, routine, or mechanical. *The cheerleaders and their* **perfunctory** *dances put our fans to sleep.*

**phlegmatic** (adjective) sluggish and unemotional in temperament. *Her performance in the dance recital was so* **phlegmatic** *that the audience forgot to clap when it was over.*

**plenary** (adjective) complete, not deficient. *The teacher said my paper was* **plenary** *with regard to facts, but she said my writing style was like that of a first grader. Yikes!*

**promulgate** (verb) to make public, to declare. *The politician waited until the day before the election to* **promulgate** *his decision to drop out of the race.*

**propriety** (noun) appropriateness.

The school board questioned the **propriety** of the music teacher dating the football coach and the janitor.

**proselytize** (verb) to attempt to make a religious or political conversion. *My grandmother thinks that rock music is trying to* **proselytize** *the youth of America.*

**protagonist** (noun) the main character in a story or play; the main supporter of an idea. *The* **protagonist** *in the movie* Braveheart *was based on a real historical figure named William Wallace.*

**pundit** (noun) someone who offers opinions in an authoritative style. *The state-champion wrestling coach has emerged as a* **pundit** *in his field.*

**Do you think the real Wallace was as hot as Mel Gibson was in the movie?**

There you go. Ten great vocab words all starting with the letter *P*. You're probably thinking that nobody will ever ask you for ten words that start with *P*. Well, think again. That might be the first question an admissions counselor will ask you when you are interviewing for college (not really). Do you know the second question she'll ask? Here it is: Can you name ten words that start with *Q?* Sure, she will.

**A plethora of *P* words. A practically perfect palette of potentially profound periphrasis. Am I wise or what?**

# Get Wise!

Fill in the blank with the appropriate word. (*Hint:* Every word used will start with the letter P. That clears things right up, doesn't it?)

**1.** The principal said her outfit lacked _____, so he made her change clothes.

**2.** The science teacher's _____ style put the entire class to sleep in 5 minutes.

**3.** The coach's _____ got him kicked out of the game.

**4.** The TV station paid the guy a fortune because they wanted a respected _____ to interview for the story.

**5.** We filed a _____ report with the company, but they still insisted on more facts and details than we provided.

**6.** His _____ study habits may prevent him from going to college.

**7.** The antagonist of the story had a serious conflict with the _____ at the climax of the story.

**8.** The school likes to _____ all the accomplishments of its students and alumni for public relations purposes.

**9.** When the chemistry teacher mixed the wrong ingredients in the lab, we all thought the lab was in jeopardy of total _____.

**10.** The earliest explorers in the New World claimed they wanted to _____ the natives when all they really wanted to do was steal the natives' riches.

## How Wise?

10. proselytize

6. phlegmatic; 7. protagonist; 8. promulgate; 9. perdition;

1. propriety; 2. perfunctory; 3. paroxysm; 4. pundit; 5. plenary;

# chapter 15

# It Would Be Wise to Watch Your Ps and Qs, Part 2

You may think you are the king or queen of vocab, but you can only claim that title if you know this quaint little list of Q words. We want you to take a quick little quiz. If you would, allow us to query you about the quantity of Q words you can come up with in 10 seconds. Let us qualify that statement by saying that Q words already used in this paragraph don't count. Ready? Go.

**One** . . .

**Two** . . .

**Three** . . .

**67**

*Get Wise! Mastering Vocabulary Skills*                    **www.petersons.com**

Four . . .

Five . . .

Six . . .

Seven . . .

Eight . . .

Nine . . .

Ten . . .

Time's up. How many did you get? That's not very many. The next time you do that exercise, make sure you can include these words in your list:

**quagmire** (noun) a bog, swamp, or bottomland. *My uncle made a bad investment when he purchased 1,000 acres of land that turned out to be a giant **quagmire**.*

**qualm** (noun) uncertainty or doubt. *I have no **qualms** about who is the best band of all time—it has to be New Kids on the Block.*

**quandary** (noun) dilemma or predicament. *The janitor created a **quandary** when he locked all his keys in the closet and couldn't unlock the school.*

**quay** (noun) pier, wharf, jetty. *In the movie* I Know What You Did Last Summer, *the cast threw a body off a **quay** and then was haunted by the person they thought was dead.*

**quell** (verb) suppress, subdue. *The coach **quelled** all rumors about his future. He announced that he was retiring to pursue a career as a taxi driver.*

**quiddity (noun) the essence or nature of something.**

The true **quiddity** of life is, uh, hmm . . . Actually, that is something that I'll have to give some more thought.

**quip** (noun) wisecrack. *The guest speaker on the economics of the school cafeteria could hardly get a word in edgewise due to all the* **quips** *from the student body.*

**quixotic** (adjective) having characteristics of Don Quixote; idealistic, extravagant, and imaginative. *The English teacher's* **quixotic** *personality inspired his students to achieve great and lofty goals.*

**quizzical** (adjective) puzzling or curious. *The cheerleader's face had a* **quizzical** *expression when she learned that there was going to be a test today.*

**quotidian** (adjective) commonplace. *The morning announcements are so* **quotidian** *that no one ever listens to them anymore.*

Speaking of *Q* words, here's something I always use when my essays are too short (and I do mean, short!): It's "*quality*, not *quantity*." Works every time!

So, how many of those words did you know? Have you heard all of them before? Did you get a quizzical look on your face when you read through the list? Surely this book hasn't become quotidian for you yet, right? Good, glad to hear it.

## Get Wise!

Match the vocab word with its synonym.

1._____ quagmire          **A.** misgiving

2._____ qualm            **B.** eccentric and idealistic

3. _____ quandary        **C.** squash or suppress

4. _____ quay            **D.** banter or crack

5. _____ quell           **E.** marsh

6. _____ quiddity        **F.** confusing

7. _____ quip            **G.** mundane

8. _____ quixotic         **H.** spirit

9. _____ quizzical        **I.** conundrum

10._____ quotidian        **J.** dock

## How Wise?

1.E; 2.A; 3.I; 4.J; 5.C; 6.H; 7.D; 8.B; 9.F; 10.G

# chapter 16

## The Wise Guys: The Newest Boy-Band Sensation

First, there were the Beatles. Years later came the New Kids on the Block. Now, for better or worse, we have 98°, Backstreet Boys, NSYNC, and O-Town. Granted, the modern music scene has its share of boy bands, but I think we need one more. That's where The Wise Guys come into the picture. Imagine, if you will, a quartet of muscle-bound boys singing and dancing to the latest beats. Now imagine the same group of verbose heartthrobs singing lyrics that use big, fancy vocab words. Sounds promising, doesn't it? We thought so, too, so when we're not writing books, we manage the newest group to hit the scene, The Wise Guys (did we mention their names already?). By day, Andrew, Micah, Jerome, and Smitty are mild-mannered guys with day jobs at a publishing company. At night, though, these guys are transformed into an enchanting new act, the likes of which the world has never seen before. To give you a preview of The Wise Guys, we have included for you some samples of their lyrics. Check these out and see what you think:

77

**contemporary** (adjective) modern, current; from the same time. *Ladies and gentlemen, let me introduce to you the hottest, most* **contemporary** *boy-band sensation, The Wise Guys, and some excerpts from their debut album.*

**corrosive** (adjective) eating away, gnawing, or destroying. *Baby, I'm sorry my temper is so explosive, but your nagging is really quite* **corrosive**.

**detractor** (noun) someone who belittles or disparages. *Baby, don't always be such a big* **detractor** *because your ring is lost in the trash compactor.*

**devious** (adjective) tricky, deceptive. *When I met you, I thought you were just mischievous, but now I know you're nothing short of* **devious**.

**elusive** (adjective) hard to capture, grasp, or understand. *The reason I'm always so* **elusive** *is that your mom is always so intrusive.*

**impeccable** (adjective) flawless. *Relax, baby, the girlies always stare at my muscles and* **impeccable** *hair.*

**remorse** (noun) a painful sense of guilt over wrongdoing. *I was filled with* **remorse** *when you left me; I guess I never should have called you "a bit too hefty."*

**timorous** (adjective) fearful, timid. *You can't be our fan if you're* **timorous**; *so choose your favorite band, either them or us.*

**validate** (verb) to officially approve or confirm. *You said you don't need a ring to* **validate** *my love for you, so instead I bought this great new baseball glove for you.*

**zealous** (adjective) filled with eagerness, fervor, or passion. *You know I tend to be a little jealous; so here's a pager, don't think I'm over* **zealous**.

**If you think these highly advanced, intellectually stimulating lyrics are appealing, you should see these guys in sequins!**

Wow! Are these guys good or what!? You should see their stage show! Bright lights, lots of smoke, a stage that looks like a giant library with laser-enhanced books. It's enough to sell out every bowling alley in every city on their tour! Look for their latest CD in the Reference section of your library, bookstore, or music store today!

# Get Wise!

Circle the word that does not belong in the word group.

**1.** new    contemporary    up-to-date    antique

**2.** erosive    corrosive    constructive    caustic

**3.** advocate    critic    detractor    censor

**4.** crafty    dimwitted    cunning    devious

**5.** elusive    evasive    slippery    obtainable

**6.** immaculate    fallible    flawless    impeccable

**7.** regret    remorse    contrition    pride

**8.** timorous    shy    sociable    fearful

**9.** verify    validate    confirm    question

**10.** ardent    spirited    apathetic    zealous

# How Wise?

1. antique; 2. constructive; 3. advocate; 4. dimwitted; 5. obtainable; 6. fallible; 7. pride; 8. sociable; 9. question; 10. apathetic

# Is It Really Wise to Have Your Head Shrunk?

Have you ever seen one of those scary, thriller-type movies about a psychologist or psychiatrist who turns out to be the freakiest person in the whole movie? You know the type we're talking about. There is some mysterious psychotic creeping around causing all sorts of problems and creating chaos for the rest of the characters in the movie. If there is a psychiatrist in the movie, you can bet the psychiatrist is the psycho. Now we're not saying all shrinks in the movies are nuts, but some of them definitely are. Maybe you've seen one of those movies recently—you decide for yourself if he or she was psycho. Either way, here are some words to consider. Perhaps you should lie down on a couch while you study these movie-friendly words:

**75**

*Get Wise! Mastering Vocabulary Skills*　　　　　　　　*www.petersons.com*

**anomaly** (noun) something different or irregular. *I paid 300 dollars an hour for him to determine that the **anomaly** in my childhood that made me this way was the death of the ants in my ant farm.*

**ascetic** (adjective) practicing strict self-discipline for moral or spiritual reasons. *If she tells you that in order to get your **ascetic** life straightened out, you should stand on your head, you should get your money back.*

**disruptive** (adjective) causing disorder, interrupting. *Dr. Smith said that my **disruptive** behavior in class is probably caused by alien communication broadcasts coming through my braces.*

**expedite** (verb) to carry out promptly. *My mom said we need to **expedite** treatment so that I don't miss the bake sale next month.*

**indistinct** (adjective) unclear, uncertain. *Every time I ask that counselor why she thinks something's wrong with me, she gives me some **indistinct** psychobabble.*

**lucid (adjective) clear and understandable.**

I painted a very **lucid** picture of my situation on the phone, and the telephone psychologist says she still doesn't have a good enough grasp of my background to make a diagnosis.

**relevance** (noun) connection to the matter at hand; pertinence. *The psychologist said that my childhood close encounter with an alien species actually has a great deal of **relevance** to my current condition.*

**sagacious** (adjective) discerning, wise. *Although I once considered the cartoon psychiatrist Dr. Katz a **sagacious** expert in his field, after seeing all of those reruns, I've recently changed my mind.*

**stimulus** (noun) something that excites a response or provokes an action. *Every time I see that ink blot, which is supposed to act as a **stimulus** for my subconscious, I can't help but think of a rhinoceros with wings.*

**suppress** (verb) to put down or restrain. *I was told once that I shouldn't suppress my feelings and that I should play charades more often. Yeah, right!*

So, how do these words make you *feel*? Did you have a happy childhood? How is your relationship with your teacher? Oops, time's up. We'll pick up here next week.

# Get Wise!

The underlined vocab words in the sentences below ended up in the *wrong* sentences. In the blank that follows each sentence, write the *correct* vocab word for that sentence.

**1.** The extra scenes that were added had absolutely no <u>stimulus</u> to the movie. _____

**2.** The monk considered himself an <u>anomaly</u>. _____

**3.** We couldn't put our finger on that <u>lucid</u> smell, but it sure was putrid. _____

**4.** The principal tried to <u>expedite</u> our opinions, but we signed a petition and made our point anyway. _____

**5.** My grandfather is the most <u>ascetic</u> man I know, probably because he has experienced so much. _____

**6.** The geeks tried to figure out the <u>relevance</u> in the computer program, but the whole server crashed anyway. _____

**7.** She gave a <u>disruptive</u> explanation, and I was able to figure out the problem with ease. _____

**8.** He was suspended because his <u>indistinct</u> comments made the teacher furious every day. _____

**9.** My sister needed a <u>sagacious</u> to wake up, so I doused her with ice water. _____

**10.** I paid for extra postage in order to <u>stimulus</u> the delivery of the sweepstakes entry form. _____

# How Wise?

1. relevance; 2. ascetic; 3. indistinct; 4. suppress; 5. sagacious; 6. anomaly; 7. lucid; 8. disruptive; 9. stimulus; 10. expedite

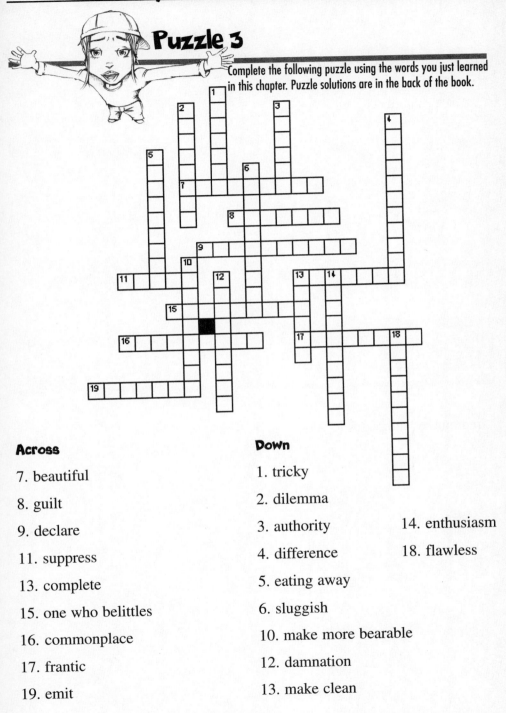

## Puzzle 3

Complete the following puzzle using the words you just learned in this chapter. Puzzle solutions are in the back of the book.

**Across**

7. beautiful

8. guilt

9. declare

11. suppress

13. complete

15. one who belittles

16. commonplace

17. frantic

19. emit

**Down**

1. tricky

2. dilemma

3. authority

4. difference

5. eating away

6. sluggish

10. make more bearable

12. damnation

13. make clean

14. enthusiasm

18. flawless

# chapter 18

## Just How Wise Are Know-It-Alls?

A smart woman once said that a man who knows much says little, while a man who knows little says much. Does that sound familiar to you? It's a safe bet that everyone knows someone who knows very little but has a whole lot to say.

You know that dude who thinks he knows everything about everything and will argue no matter what the subject is and no matter whom he's arguing with at the time? That kind of person isn't unique. And they're all on the football team!

**87**

*Get Wise! Mastering Vocabulary Skills*                    www.petersons.com

For some reason, there are more people like that than you might think. These arguers would probably argue with the best baseball player in the National League or single-handedly take on the top debate team from an Ivy League if he were given the opportunity. A psychologist would probably say that this condition, *disgruntledargumentativitis*, was due to some chemical imbalance. Practically speaking, this is just that plain old hardheadedness your grandmother used to talk about. Here are some words that could very easily be connected with these argumentative know-it-alls:

**arbitrary** (adjective) based on random or merely personal preference. *Does that guy argue about everything, or does he just pick* **arbitrary** *subjects to argue about?*

**digress** (verb) to wander from the main path or the main topic. *If you get into an argument with a know-it-all, try to* **digress** *and get off the subject so you can get away from him as soon as possible!*

**exculpate** (verb) to free from blame or guilt. *Know-it-alls always seem to* **exculpate** *themselves after an argument by convincing themselves that they are right and everyone else is wrong, way wrong.*

**feral** (adjective) wild. *Some know-it-alls turn* **feral** *if they are embarrassed in front of their friends.*

**nocturnal** (adjective) of the night; active at night. *Argumentative know-it-alls would do well to be* **nocturnal** *creatures who stay up all night and study; unfortunately, most don't know anything.*

**proficient** (adjective) skillful, adept.

Few know-it-alls are as **proficient** at arguing as the cafeteria lady who actually convinced us that the food was fat-free and calorie-free.

**repudiate** (verb) to reject, to renounce. *If you say the sky is blue and the grass is green, you can bet your last dollar that a know-it-all will* **repudiate** *your statement.*

**sustain** (verb) to keep up, to continue; to support. *There was actually a study once that said some people are born with a genetic defect that allows them to* **sustain** *an argument indefinitely.*

**untenable** (adjective) impossible to defend. *Know-it-alls will argue to the death even over* **untenable** *points or positions.*

**unyielding** (adjective) firm, resolute, obdurate. *Never argue with know-it-alls. They are always hard-headed,* **unyielding**, *stubborn, and certain that they are right and you are wrong!*

**One night when I was looking for the radio station that was supposed to be playing Weezer all day and all night, I heard some guy on a talk station calling another guy *untenable, unyielding,* and *feral.* I certainly didn't know what he was talking about, but it sounded like a pretty good fight! I never did find that Weezer station, but I digress.**

On second thought, know-it-alls aren't so bad sometimes. You have to admit that when the English teacher and the know-it-all get into an argument about the real meaning of some poem you never heard of, it can be very entertaining!

## Get Wise!

Match the vocabulary word with its antonym.

1. _____ arbitrary          A. unskilled

2. _____ digress            B. flexible

3. _____ exculpate          C. defensible

4. _____ feral              D. selectively chosen

5. _____ nocturnal          E. linger

6. _____ proficient         F. tame

7. _____ repudiate          G. discontinue

8. _____ sustain            H. diurnal

9. _____ untenable          I. accept

10. _____ unyielding        J. convict

I know other people like that, but I'm quite sure I'm not at all like that. And if you don't believe me, just ask me and I'll *make* you agree with me!

## How Wise?

1. D; 2. E; 3. J; 4. F; 5. H; 6. A; 7. I; 8. G; 9. C; 10. B

# A Wise Investment?

We're going to date ourselves again with the beginning of this chapter, but we guess we can live with that. A few, well, several years ago . . . OK, a long time ago, back when Tom Hanks was a nobody in Hollywood, he made a movie called *The Money Pit*. Hanks's character in the movie bought a run-down old house and intended to fix it up. The house was a disaster and should have been condemned. Finally, after dozens of hilarious (at least for the audience) disasters and a lot of money down the drain, Hanks's character fixes up the house and restores it to its original, beautiful condition. What's the point? We know somebody who once bought a house that needed a little cosmetic work. Well, actually it was a dump, but it seemed promising. We mean, it sounded like a good idea at the time. Anyway, here are a few words that reminded us of that fateful investment:

**85**

*Get Wise! Mastering Vocabulary Skills*          www.petersons.com

**Tom Hanks? Wasn't he the guy in that movie who talked to the volleyball for 4 hours? Talk about nuts!**

**auspicious** (adjective) promising good fortune; propitious. *The horseshoe hanging over the front door of my new house seemed like an **auspicious** sign until it fell on my head and gave me a concussion.*

**durable** (adjective) long lasting. *Still reeling from my knock on the head, I stumbled inside and leaned on the **durable** stone fireplace; much to my chagrin, the fireplace collapsed and the stones fell on my foot, breaking three of my toes.*

**exacerbate** (verb) to make worse or more severe. *Then, when I thought things couldn't get any worse, dozens of bats flew down the chimney and **exacerbated** the entire situation.*

**expropriate** (verb) to seize ownership of. *The house was in such a state of disrepair that I feared the building commissioner would **expropriate** the property at any time.*

**formidable** (adjective) awesome, impressive, or frightening.

At this point, facing a most **formidable** task, I decided to call Bob Vila (you know, that guy on TV who fixes up old houses on that show your grandparents watch all the time). Well, he said, "No way!"

**refurbish** (verb) to fix up; renovate. *At that point, I decided to **refurbish** the property myself.*

**renovate** (verb) to renew by repairing or rebuilding. *Why didn't someone tell me how hard it is to **renovate** a house?*

**strenuous** (adjective) requiring energy and strength. *After thousands and thousands of dollars and months of* **strenuous** *work on the house, the unthinkable happened.*

**unparalleled** (adjective) with no equal; unique. *Three weeks before I was scheduled to complete the renovations, a tornado of* **unparalleled** *proportions sucked up my house and dropped it somewhere in west Texas. No, really, it did!*

**vestige** (noun) a trace or remainder. *Now the last* **vestiges** *of what was once my house are a pile of stones where the fireplace once stood (and fell) and a horseshoe stuck in a tree.*

Now, before you start feeling too sorry for the guy, the insurance company decided to write him a big check to cover the loss of the house. You know what he did? He ran right out and bought another fixer-upper with the insurance check! It was kind of rundown, but it showed a lot of promise. We think we heard he's going to renovate the house himself! Is he kidding?

**They say a man's home is his castle. Well, I have a feeling this castle is going to end up in ruins.**

# Get Wise!

Fill in the blank in each sentence with the correct vocab word.

1. The teacher decided to _____ the student's candy because the teacher was a big ogre who would eat anything that wasn't nailed down.

2. Today's PE class was the most _____ class ever. We had to walk around the track for 15 minutes! What a workout!!

3. Maybe one day they will _____ our school and get rid of the lime green, nauseous pink, and institutional blue paint on all the walls.

4. When our star player dunked the ball after the tipoff of the first game, we all saw that as an _____ sign. Unfortunately, he landed wrong and broke his ankle, and we lost every game that season.

5. We already had a tyrant for a principal; then, to _____ matters, the principal hired an ex-Marine drill sergeant as the assistant principal!

6. A dismal Celebrity Boxing performance is the last _____ of the once-promising career of Vanilla Ice.

7. Rumor has it that the school is going to _____ the cheerleaders' locker room in the offseason; they are going to add a dozen extra mirrors, hair-spray dispensers, lipstick vending machines, and a big pompom holder.

8. My math book is so _____; I have used it to prop open doors, to jack up my car when it had a flat, to practice shooting my crossbow at, to hold all my pens and papers, and to kill roaches in the cafeteria.

9. My mom always proves to be a _____ opponent because she always knows when I get a bad grade, when I'm out after curfew, and when I'm not exactly telling the whole truth.

10. Marilyn Manson is a guy whose weirdness is simply _____.

## How Wise?

1. expropriate; 2. strenuous; 3. refurbish; 4. auspicious; 5. exacerbate; 6. vestige; 7. renovate; 8. durable; 9. formidable; 10. unparalleled

# chapter 20

## Infomercial Products: A Wise Buy?

It's 2:30 a.m. on a Saturday and you're aimlessly flipping TV channels. Other than some cookie-cutter woman-in-trouble movie on the Lifetime Network, the only shows on the other channels are infomercials. As if all the shop-from-your-couch channels weren't bad enough, companies are buying huge chunks of air time to run infomercials to convince you that you need a Chia Pet or an Abdominizer or a Thigh Blaster or a contraption that dehydrates entire meals and removes all the fat, calories, cholesterol, and flavor from the food. These infomercials shamelessly promote everything from solar-powered flashlights to "Make a Million Dollars in Ten Days for only $19.99" videotapes. Believe it or not, though, these infomercials actually do have some value in our society. Just imagine all the out-of-work actors and actresses who would still be out of work if it weren't for the infomercials!

89

*Get Wise! Mastering Vocabulary Skills*                    *www.petersons.com*

You know, if you can't memorize all this vocab, and you can't pass your tests, and you can't get into college, there are always infomercials!

**affected** (adjective) false, artificial. *I knew the spokeswoman was giving an **affected** sales pitch when she claimed that you could lose fifteen pounds and have six-pack abs overnight by simply wearing a specially magnetized T-shirt that polarizes fat cells and drives the fat from your body.*

**ardor** (noun) a strong feeling of passion, energy, or zeal. *The over-the-hill fitness guru pitched his product with such **ardor** that I almost believed I could become taller by sleeping suspended upside down from his Height Enhancer machine.*

**caustic** (adjective) burning, corrosive. *The beautiful supermodel failed to read the fine print on the Doctor Hair-B-Gone hair removal system that warned of the **caustic** sensation caused by the product, especially under the nose. Ouch!*

**dissipate** (verb) to spread out or scatter. *The spokesperson claimed that the Household Odor Deodorizer would **dissipate** only seconds after it was sprayed in the house and would neutralize any and all household odors, even disgusting diaper pail odors, for the next ten years.*

**elated** (adjective) excited and happy; exultant. *The "actual satisfied customer" who sounds so **elated** on the phone on all the infomercials is probably just the same actress who specializes in that kind of work.*

**gratuitous** (adjective) given freely or without cause. *One of my favorite things about infomercials is the thousands of dollars' worth of **gratuitous** gifts that companies offer at no additional charge (except for the $24.95 shipping and handling fee).*

**mandate** (noun) order, command. *Some infomercials are so successful that I wonder if there are subliminal **mandates** hidden in the infomercial music that make people want to buy worthless junk.*

**obsolete** (adjective) no longer current; old-fashioned.

My dad bought a computer from an infomercial because the spokespeople convinced him that his computer was obsolete. Then they convinced him to buy an upgrade package because the computer he had just purchased would be **obsolete** by the time he got off the phone with them.

**talisman** (noun) an object supposed to have magical effects or qualities. *My all-time favorite infomercial product is the Ancient Navajo Indian **talisman** made of fool's gold that, if worn on the forehead of the purchaser, protects the purchaser from making foolish decisions.*

**tranquillity** (noun) freedom from disturbance or turmoil; calm. *I once saw an infomercial selling a potion that, when used as a shampoo, instantly transformed a person's mood from manic-depression to **tranquillity**.*

# Get Wise!

Match the vocab word with its synonym.

1. _____ affected            A. peace

2. _____ ardor               B. disintegrate

3. _____ caustic             C. extra

4. _____ dissipate           D. insincere

5. _____ elated              E. charm

6. _____ gratuitous          F. antiquated

7. _____ mandate             G. overjoyed

8. _____ obsolete            H. order

9. _____ talisman            I. zeal

10. _____ tranquillity        J. stinging

# How Wise?

1. D; 2. I; 3. J; 4. B; 5. G; 6. C; 7. H; 8. F; 9. E; 10. A

# chapter 21

## Wise Words from Country Music

Maybe boy bands don't do anything for you and you are more of a country music fan. If so, then you'll appreciate this chapter. If you're not a country music fan, pay attention and you may learn something. Let us first make an observation. The majority of real country music songs are about:

* ★ trucks

* ★ a dog

* ★ a farm

* ★ bad luck

* ★ significant others who cheat

* ★ or honky-tonks (that's country talk for a night club)

93

*Get Wise! Mastering Vocabulary Skills*                    *www.petersons.com*

If you are an avid country music listener, you know there are a few more things about which songs are written. But we were told that we really can't get into those topics in this book. Anyway, in the spirit of down-on-their-luck cowboys, we put together a few lines that someone might want to borrow for their country music songs. If anyone out there is interested, simply contact the publisher for information on how to procure our services. Just kidding!

**While you read these ridiculous lyrics, just try to imagine Tim McGraw or The Dixie Chicks singing `em. Maybe that'll help you get through the list. On the other hand, maybe it won't.**

**arable** (adjective) able to be cultivated for growing crops. *I'm down on my luck and my life's been terrible since my dog ran off and my farm's not* **arable**.

**capricious** (adjective) unpredictable, willful, whimsical. *I love my cowgirl, she's wild and* **capricious***, she likes big trucks and she hunts and she fishes.*

**fractious** (adjective) troublesome, unruly. *Here's a more intellectual way to remake the Hank Williams, Jr. classic: I got the pig in the ground, I got some drinks on ice, and all my* **fractious** *friends are comin' over tonight.*

**glutton** (noun) one who is overly hungry for something. *I like my woman, but she sure is a* **glutton***. She just ate a chicken and a barbecued mutton.*

**impute** (verb) to credit or give responsibility to; to attribute. *To that cowboy much gratitude I do* **impute***, he found my lost gator-skin cowboy boot.*

**induce** (verb) to cause. *Somehow that guitar (pronounced git-tar) can magically* **induce** *a fit of dancin', partyin', and cuttin' loose.*

**parsimony** (noun) stinginess, miserly behavior. *My mean ole wife's so full of* **parsimony***; she wants my horse, my truck, and lots of alimony.*

**peruse** (verb) to examine or study. *I stood and* **perused** *the music in the jukebox. Then I saw her and thought, "Wow, what a fox!"*

**scoff** (verb) mock or make fun of. *Rednecks like me just love to* **scoff** *at well-dressed guys who like to play golf.*

**terse** (adjective) concise, brief to the point of being rude. *Please don't think I'm* **terse***, it's just a short verse.*

I wonder if these geeks sing just as bad as they write?

We have a great idea to help you study this list of words. We know you've been using the flashcards, right? Good. Don't stop using them. To really get into the spirit for this chapter, go to the gas station on the corner and buy one of those really cheap cassette tapes of George Jones or Loretta Lynn that they keep on the counter. Then put on your boots and listen to the tape while you study these words. Ya'll have fun now, ya hear?

I think these people should stick to writing books, ya think?

# Get Wise!

The underlined vocab words in the sentences below are in the *wrong* sentences. In the blank that follows each sentence, write the *correct* vocab word for that sentence.

**1.** The fans always <u>impute</u> at the officials during basketball games. _____

**2.** Her <u>induce</u> behavior makes her seem immature and much younger than she actually is. _____

**3.** The food critic was an admitted <u>parsimony</u>, and that's why he liked his job so much. _____

**4.** His <u>glutton</u> resulted in a huge savings account after only a few years. _____

**5.** People once thought rock music had the power to <u>capricious</u> all sorts of strange behavior in teenagers. _____

**6.** Desert property doesn't bring a high price because it usually isn't <u>fractious</u>. _____

**7.** Blink 182 has a reputation as one of the most <u>terse</u> bands when they stay in hotels. _____

**8.** She's just shy and socially inept. Many people don't know that, and they think she is always <u>arable</u>. _____

**9.** I could stand in the music store and <u>scoff</u> the CDs for hours. _____

**10.** I try hard not to <u>peruse</u> resentment toward him even though he did steal my girlfriend, win prom king, and make the varsity baseball team over me. _____

## How Wise?

1. scoff; 2. capricious; 3. glutton; 4. parsimony; 5. induce; 6. arable; 7. fractious; 8. terse; 9. peruse; 10. impute

*Get Wise! Mastering Vocabulary Skills*

# chapter 22

# Words to Make Your Music Teacher Think You're Wise (Sort of)

**That country music in the last chapter has made me want to think about some *other* kinds of music, any music, immediately! Please?**

Ok, Chi, do you know how to play the piano or some other instrument? Do you have to go to some kind of music lessons every day or every week? If

**97**

*Get Wise! Mastering Vocabulary Skills*                    *www.petersons.com*

so, hang in there. One day, those tuba lessons will pay off. Anyway, we have some good words for you to add to your music vocabulary. You can use these words the way your music teacher might use them, or you can be a little more creative. Study this list and you'll see what we mean:

**asthetic** (adjective) beautiful, pleasing, or artistic. *Metallica's joint effort with the San Francisco Symphony Orchestra actually had a terrific balance of edge and* **aesthetic** *appeal.*

**baroque** (adjective) very ornate, flowery, and ornamental. *Korn does not qualify as* **baroque** *music; they just let it rip.*

**cacophony** (noun) discord or dissonance. *Rage Against the Machine often uses* **cacophony** *in its music, thus giving it a distorted, busy sound.*

**improvisation** (noun) impromptu extemporization. *Run DMC and the Fat Boys, grandfathers of modern rap, were masters of* **improvisation.**

**lyrical** (adjective) sweet and musical. *The movie* Moulin Rouge *was a* **lyrical** *adventure set in Paris many years ago.*

**maestro** (noun) a master of a trade, a virtuoso. *Kid Rock might be considered a* **maestro** *because no one else does his type of music the way he does.*

**muse (noun) one who inspires art, especially music.**

Was J-Lo ever the **muse** for any of P-Diddy's music?

**opus** (noun) a grand musical composition; metaphor for a great achievement. *"Stairway to Heaven" might be considered Led Zeppelin's* **opus.**

**symphonic** (adjective) melodious, harmonious. *Some girls claim they like* *N SYNC for their* **symphonic** *music, but we all know that girls like *N SYNC because they think the guys are hot.*

**virtuoso** (noun) someone very skilled, especially in an art. *Jimi Hendrix may have been the greatest rock guitar* **virtuoso** *of all time.*

I bet you thought they were going to write about Barry Manilow and the Bee Gees. Frankly, so did I.

Obviously, these vocab words can be used with the classical music like Bach, Beethoven, Handel, and Wagner, but it sure would be more fun to tell your music teacher about Limp Bizkit, Ozzy Osbourne, Creed, and Staind, don't you think?

Ever heard that song "Roll Over Beethoven"? Well, if Beethoven knew how these words were being used, he'd roll over in his grave!

# Get Wise!

Circle the word in each of the following word groups that does not belong.

**1.** unappealing      aesthetic      pleasant      tasteful

**2.** frilly      rococo      baroque      plain

**3.** cacophony      chaos      disorder      harmony

**4.** invention      innovation      choreography improvisation

**5.** dulcet      lyrical      silvery      disharmonious

**6.** master      maestro      novice      expert

**7.** incubus      vision      inspiration      muse

**8.** piece      opus      failure      composition

**9.** tuneful      symphonic      sonorous      chaotic

**10.** maestro      apprentice      genius      virtuoso

# How Wise?

# Puzzle 4

Complete the following puzzle using the words you just learned in this chapter. Puzzle solutions are in the back of the book.

**Across**

2. renovate
6. to keep up
7. clear
8. irregularity
10. carry out
11. wild
12. long lasting
16. unclear
18. remainder
19. discerning
20. pertinence

**Down**

1. propitious
3. free from guilt
4. to seize
5. unequaled
9. renounce
13. active at night
14. wander
15. indefensible
17. put down

# chapter 23

# It Wouldn't Be Wise to Take This Guy Home to Meet the Parents

The other day in the mall, we saw some dude wearing a T-shirt that said, "I'm the guy your mom warned you about." At first we thought the guy just wanted some attention. On closer inspection, though, we started believing that he knew exactly what he was talking about. Close your eyes and picture this guy in your mind as we describe him in the sentences that follow. (We may not have tricked *you*, but you know there is some kid somewhere out there who is sitting with her eyes closed wondering how she is supposed to read the sentences and keep her eyes closed at the same time.) Seriously, picture this guy. He was about 5'10" but almost 6'0" if you measure to the top of his mullet. He was wearing faded jeans with a to-

**103**

*Get Wise! Mastering Vocabulary Skills*      *www.petersons.com*

bacco can ring in one back pocket and a red bandanna in the other back pocket. His shirt (you already know what his shirt said) was washed and dried a few too many times, and it stretched tightly across his belly, which hung over his way-too-tight jeans. Did I mention his mullet? Finally, his sleeves were rolled up to expose a "Bobby Ray" tattoo on one arm and a "Van Halen Rocks" tattoo on the other. We think this really was the guy your mom warned you about!

**If you ever showed an interest in this freak, your parents would probably send you to a convent or boarding school!**

**cognizant** (adjective) aware, mindful. *Don't bring home a guy who makes your parents wonder through the entire dinner if he is even* **cognizant** *of his surroundings.*

**hedonist** (noun) someone who lives mainly to pursue pleasure. *Don't bring home a* **hedonist** *who tells your parents his goal is to "eat, drink, and be merry."*

**incoherent** (adjective) unable to be understood. *Don't bring home a guy whose speech is* **incoherent** *and who will mumble through the entire dinner.*

**inebriated** (adjective) intoxicated. *Don't ever bring home a guy who is* **inebriated** *if you want to make a good impression on your parents.*

**innate (adjective) inborn, native.**

Don't bring home a guy who has an **innate** desire to belch and make fart sounds in his armpits.

**insolence** (noun) an attitude or behavior that is bold and disrespectful. *Don't bring home a brown-noser, but don't bring home a guy who will act with* **insolence** *toward your mother.*

**irate** (adjective) enraged. *Don't bring home a guy who will get* **irate** *if your parents ask where he plans to take you after the dance.*

**neurotic** (adjective) disturbed, unstable, deranged. *Don't bring home a* **neurotic** *guy who might do something like steal your dog or kiss your mom before you go out for the evening.*

**presumptuous** (adjective) going beyond the limits of courtesy or appropriateness. *Don't bring home a guy who would be* **presumptuous** *enough to call your parents "Mike and Carol" or "June and Ward."*

**profane** (adjective) irreverent or vulgar. *Don't bring home a guy who uses* **profane** *language. If you do bring him home, just make sure he doesn't open his mouth.*

**Ladies, did you recognize any of these guys? Guys, did any of these hit too close to home?**

We're quite sure that none of you would ever be seen with old Bobby Ray or any of the other guys described above. Then again, there is that old adage that says there is someone for everyone! Maybe he's the one for you!

# Get Wise!

Match each vocab word with its antonym.

| | | | |
|---|---|---|---|
| 1. _____ | cognizant | A. | sober |
| 2. _____ | hedonist | B. | respect |
| 3. _____ | incoherent | C. | conservative |
| 4. _____ | inebriated | D. | reserved |
| 5. _____ | innate | E. | learned |
| 6. _____ | insolence | F. | balanced |
| 7. _____ | irate | G. | holy |
| 8. _____ | neurotic | H. | unaware |
| 9. _____ | presumptuous | I. | calm |
| 10. _____ | profane | J. | clear |

# How Wise?

1. H; 2. C; 3. J; 4. A; 5. E; 6. B; 7. I; 8. F; 9. D; 10. G

# chapter 24

## Sometimes It Is Wise to Use Four-Letter Words, Part 1

What do you think of when someone says "four-letter word"? Yep, that's what we thought. All those four-letter words out there—you just can't get away from them. Music, movies, the hallways at school are all filled with those choice four-letter words that will land you in detention or get your mouth washed out with soap (if you're at your grandmother's house!). We don't know about you, but when we hear people throwing around those four-letter words, we always wonder if those people's vocabularies are just so small that they just don't know any other words to use. What a shame! You know, there are actually plenty of good, quality four-letter words out there just waiting to be used. Now don't think for one #@!* second that we're going to teach you some more $@#! words to throw around. Nope. We're just going to learn some good four-letter vocab words. We mean, seriously, do you think we're that irresponsible? Nope. Let's look at some really good four-letter vocab:

**107**

*Get Wise! Mastering Vocabulary Skills*                    www.petersons.com

**acme** (noun) the highest point of achievement or development. *Unfortunately for the baseball team, he reached the* **acme** *of his career in the same game in which he threw out his arm.*

**avid** (adjective) having a great interest or enthusiasm. *She is an* **avid** *reader of both* Big Hair Magazine *and* New Makeup Ideas Magazine.

**cant** (noun) hypocritical language; empty talk. *The principal has been giving a lot of* **cant** *to the discussion on reserved parking for seniors, but we all know he is just bluffing.*

**coup** (noun) takeover of power or a leadership position. *The tee-ball team staged a* **coup** *and replaced the fat, old coach with the second baseman's 17- year-old sister.*

**dreg** (noun) the lowest or least desirable (often used as plural *dregs*). *Although he once was a* **dreg** *of the school's social scene, he worked out all summer and now he's the hottest guy in the eleventh grade.*

**fiat** (noun) order or decree. *The cheerleading sponsor's greatest* **fiat** *was "Never stop smiling."*

**flay** (verb) to strip the skin; to harshly criticize. *As an intimidation tactic, the ancient Assyrians* **flayed** *their enemies. I'm intimidated, and they've all been dead for thousands of years!*

**glib** (adjective) performed with ease. *Her exaggerations have become so* **glib** *that we fear she may be a pathological liar.*

**mien** (noun) manner that reveals a state of mind.

Rob Zombie's **mien** makes one wonder if he had some sort of traumas that make him the way he is now.

**oust** (verb) to eject. *The chess club members threatened to* **oust** *their president if he lost a match to anyone who was not in the chess club.*

The tough thing about four-letter vocab words, the ones you'll learn here anyway, is that there may not always be discernible word parts to help you figure out the meaning of the word. The best way to handle these four-letter words is just to memorize them. Remember your flashcards?

# Get Wise!

In each of the following sentences, fill in the blank with the correct vocab word.

1. You know your teacher needs a vacation when her biting sarcasm becomes so _____ that she's rude to everyone she meets.

2. An _____ fisherman, he once tried to catch the carp in the fountain at the Chinese restaurant.

3. It's sad that the movie *Shazam* was the _____ of Shaq's acting career.

4. A leader should not give a _____ that he or she is not prepared to follow, too.

5. The people of Boobooland, a small, remote, country, are threatening to _____ their dictator and replace him with a witch doctor.

**6.** The news has just reported that the Booboolandian people staged a _____ and seized control of the government complex in the capital city.

**7.** The geometry teacher threatened to _____ anyone who was caught cheating on one of her impossible exams.

**8.** The bank robber's _____ seemed to indicate that robbing the bank was an act of desperation.

**9.** A person should not use _____ when talking about serious subjects.

**10.** The lady who always talks to herself hasn't always been a _____ of society; she once was a grammarian who lost her mind when she found a sentence she couldn't diagram.

**How Wise?**

1. glib; 2. avid; 3. acme; 4. flat; 5. oust; 6. coup; 7. flay; 8. mien; 9. cant; 10. dreg

# Sometimes It Is Wise to Use Four-Letter Words, Part 2

So have you told your friends that you learned some new four-letter words? What? Your friends don't know that you are actually deeply absorbed in this page-turner of a book? We bet you told them that your parents are making you read this book and that they are making you study those flash-cards. It's OK to let people know your all-time favorite book is this vo-cabulary book. In fact, it would be OK to share the book with your friends, that is, if you don't wear out the cover before you finish reading it for the third time. Enough about your obsession with this book. Let's do some more vocab—that's what you want, right?

**111**

*Get Wise! Mastering Vocabulary Skills*                    *www.petersons.com*

Are these people for real? They can't be serious. Like you are only going to read this three times! I know I'm going to read it at least five times! Yeah, right.

**pall** (noun) a covering that darkens or hides. *The winless football season cast a **pall** over the school for the rest of the semester.*

**rash** (adjective) marked by ill-conceived haste. *Her rash decision to wear her friend's shoes resulted in a nasty **rash** on her feet that wouldn't go away.*

**rife** (adjective) in abundance or great numbers.

My auto shop class is **rife** with preps and geeks due to a computer's scheduling error; this should be interesting.

**saga** (noun) a long prose narrative. *The documentation of all the problems on the boys' baseball team reads like a **saga**.*

**sage** (noun) a person of great wisdom. *My grandfather is like a **sage** because he always knows what to say when I need advice.*

**taut** (adjective) tense, strained. *The **taut** expression on his face indicated that he totally forgot to study for the test.*

**tyro** (noun) a beginner. *With a little practice, even a **tyro** can learn to drive a car.*

**wane** (verb) to decrease in size, intensity, or quantity. *Her interest in becoming class president began to **wane** when she learned that she would actually have responsibilities, obligations, and duties.*

**wary** (adjective) cautious or watchful. *I was **wary** of the guy on the phone when he said I had won a trip around the world with no strings attached.*

**whet** (verb) sharpen or make more acute. *Always remember to use a **whet** rock to sharpen your scissors before you cut your hair ribbons.*

Well, there you go. Maybe you already knew some of these four-letter words, but I bet you didn't know all of them. Just remember the best way to deal with most words like this is simply to memorize them. There isn't exactly a plethora of difficult words of five letters or less, so you would do well just to learn them, instead of relying on vocab skills to decipher them.

# Get Wise!

Match the vocab word with its synonym.

| | | |
|---|---|---|
| 1. _____ pall | | A. diminish |
| 2. _____ rash | | B. rigid |
| 3. _____ rife | | C. alert |
| 4. _____ saga | | D. epic |
| 5. _____ sage | | E. heedless |
| 6. _____ taut | | F. hone |
| 7. _____ tyro | | G. prevalent |
| 8. _____ wane | | H. philosopher |
| 9. _____ wary | | I. shadow |
| 10. _____ whet | | J. novice |

# How Wise?

1. I; 2. E; 3. G; 4. D; 5. H; 6. B; 7. J; 8. A; 9. C; 10. F

# Wise Words about Using Words

When it comes to using words, whether in speaking or writing, there are varying degrees to which you can use words. You can be short and to the point. You can ramble on and on just to hear yourself speak or read your own writing or just see how many words you can fit between a capital letter and a punctuation mark without creating a dreaded run-on sentence for which you could receive a failing grade if you have a mean teacher like a couple of the teachers we had when we were in high school! See what we mean? For each and every possible number of words a person uses and the way in which they are used, there is a word to describe that usage. Enough of the babbling, you'll see what we mean:

**115**

*Get Wise! Mastering Vocabulary Skills*                    *www.petersons.com*

Phew! Are we done yet? Guess I get your point . . . we should make our point and fast!

**concise** (adjective) expressed briefly and simply; succinct. *I decided to answer the essay question with a* **concise** *statement: I DON'T KNOW.*

**delineate** (verb) to outline or describe. *My plan is to* **delineate** *the proposed policies in my campaign speech.*

**diatribe** (noun) bitter, biting speech. *The once-genial campaign speech turned into a harsh* **diatribe***.*

**incisive (adjective) expressed clearly and directly.**

If the teacher had written **incisive** directions, then the entire class wouldn't have screwed up the assignment.

**jargon** (noun) language or terminology associated with something particular. *Lawyers are the world's worst at using* **jargon** *that the average person can't possibly understand.*

**preamble** (noun) an introductory statement. *The* **preamble** *to his book said in 200 words what the rest of the book took 200 pages to say.*

**sequential** (adjective) arranged in an order or series. *Unless you want to really confuse the audience, always deliver your speech in a* **sequential** *manner.*

**substantiated** (adjective) verified or supported by evidence. *If a research paper is not* **substantiated***, then it is nothing more than speculation.*

**rhetoric** (noun) insincere, hollow writing or speech. *Politicians are notorious for filling their speeches with* **rhetoric**.

**verbose** (adjective) excessively wordy. *I don't like* **verbose** *sentences.*

Words about words. If you can say it or write it, there is a word to describe either what you say or the way you say it. These words, unlike some of the vocab that gets tested on standardized exams, are words you can actually use in everyday situations.

# Get Wise!

Circle the word in each of the following word groups that does not belong.

**1.** condensed    short    concise    expanded

**2.** delineate    describe    disguise    outline

**3.** diatribe    applause    denunciation    harangue

**4.** incisive    ambiguous    clear-cut    sharp

**5.** lingo    jargon    idiom    antonym

**6.** introduction    prologue    epilogue    preamble

**7.** orderly    insubsequent    sequential    chronological

**8.** unfounded    supported    demonstrable    substantiated

**9.** bravado    oration    rhetoric    silence

**10.** verbose    wordy    brief    loquacious

## How Wise?

1. expanded; 2. disguise; 3. applause; 4. ambiguous; 5. antonym; 6. epilogue; 7. insubsequent; 8. unfounded; 9. silence; 10. brief

# chapter 27

# Words of Wisdom for the Next Time You Call a Plumber

**These people have lost their minds! Would you agree?**

Stay with us. Just remember that you'll be in college in a couple of years. You may be in a dorm, you may be in an apartment, or you may be baby-sitting in someone's house. One day, you just wait and see, you are going to have a problem that's going to require a plumber. Believe us when we tell

**119**

*Get Wise! Mastering Vocabulary Skills*                    www.petersons.com

you, there is nothing more embarrassing or more frustrating than having to call a plumber, then telling him that you know exactly what the problem is, only to have him come to the house and discover that the problem is something else. For example, imagine calling the plumber and saying that your toilet is stopped up. You tell him that it is probably just too much toilet tissue in the toilet. The plumber comes over and, much to your dismay, he discovers that there is a shirt stuck in the toilet's pipes. Then you have to confess to your roommate that you borrowed her shirt, got a stain on it, and tried to flush it so that you didn't have to admit that you took the shirt without asking. Really, it could happen and you better be prepared!

Did you know that the guy who invented the toilet was named John Crapper? Seriously! Go look it up!

**alienate** (verb) to estrange. *You might **alienate** the plumber if you laugh when he bends over and shows you a little more than you wanted to see.*

**convoluted** (adjective) twisting, complicated, intricate. *There is a **convoluted** maze of sewage pipes under our house, which means that there are many places for stuff (you know) to get stopped up.*

**discern** (verb) to detect, notice, or observe. *Without a professional plumber, it may be impossible to **discern** exactly why that stuff is coming out of the drain in the tub.*

**diverge** (verb) to move in different directions. *You may never find your mom's antique ring that you accidentally flushed down the toilet, because the pipes **diverge** under the house and head out toward two different septic tanks.*

**inconsequential** (adjective) of little importance. *It seemed **inconsequential** at the time, but now that the toilet is stopped up, I am a little worried about my missing harmonica.*

**jeopardize** (verb) to put in danger. *The plumber said that an exploding toilet may* **jeopardize** *the apartment below ours.*

**revere** (verb) to admire deeply, to honor. *I began to* **revere** *the plumber more than I could have imagined when I saw him put his hand way down in the toilet and retrieve the Rolex that I borrowed from my dad.*

**stagnate** (verb) to become stale through lack of movement or change. *Apparently our faucet leaked so badly that our downstairs neighbors' apartment flooded and formed a big pool of water that began to* **stagnate** *while they were on vacation.*

**surreptitious** (adjective) done in secret. *I made sure my call to the plumber was* **surreptitious** *because if my parents found out that I flushed my little brother's toy down the toilet, I would be so dead meat.*

**tentative** (adjective) subject to change; uncertain. *I was a little* **tentative** *about opening the lid to the toilet when I heard sounds coming from inside the basin.*

We hope you aren't feeling too flushed after reading those sentences. We had some even more disgusting sentences, but we were told, "Your sentences stink," and then we had to rewrite them. Hopefully this book won't make a great writing career go down the drain.

# Get Wise!

The underlined vocab words in the sentences below are in the *wrong* sentences. On the line that follows each sentence, write the *correct* vocab word for that sentence.

1.  The fact that the Congressman has two speeding tickets seems <u>convoluted</u> in light of his arrest for espionage. _____

2.  Two roads <u>jeopardize</u> in a neighborhood, and I didn't know which way to go. _____

**3.** His story was so <u>inconsequential</u> that the principal had no idea if he was telling the truth or not. _____

**4.** The <u>tentative</u> actions of the chess club eventually led to serious situations, like the time they tried to use a nonregulation board in a competition. Those wild and crazy guys! _____

**5.** He didn't want to <u>diverged</u> his career as a surfer, so he always made sure his hair was bleached blond. _____

**6.** The fastest way to <u>convoluted</u> some is to ask them to leave your presence immediately. _____

**7.** Without my glasses, I couldn't <u>revere</u> the difference between the cheerleader and the mascot. _____

**8.** A very <u>surreptitious</u> person would never make it on a show like "Fear Factor." _____

**9.** If you let a sink full of water <u>discern</u> long enough, you don't have to think very hard about what to do for your science project.

_____

**10.** You have to <u>stagnate</u> that guy named Paul who rode around saying "the British are coming." If it weren't for him, the Beatles would have taken America by surprise. _____

# How Wise?

1. inconsequential; 2. diverge; 3. convoluted; 4. surreptitious; 5. jeopardize; 6. alienate; 7. discern; 8. tentative; 9. stagnate; 10. revere

# Puzzle 5

Complete the following puzzle using the words you just learned in this chapter. Puzzle solutions are in the back of the book.

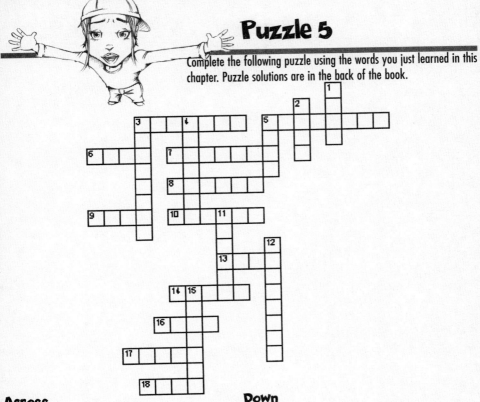

## Across

3. arrogant

5. bitter speech

6. in abundance

7. short

8. terminology

9. dark covering

10. friendly

13. pinnacle

14. envy

16. takeover

17. enraged

18. empty talk

## Down

1. cautious

2. wise man

3. introduction

4. vulgar

5. lowest of society

11. inborn

12. disturbed

15. lavish

# chapter 28

## A Wise Person Knows All That Glitters Isn't Gold

There's another one of those sayings similar to something a *sagacious* (remember this word?) old man like Confucius might say. Basically it means that everything that is shiny and glittery and glamorous isn't necessarily precious. But you knew that already. We guess a more modern and practical application of this is to say that money does not buy happiness. We don't know about you, but we do kind of agree with this. However, we're pretty sure that although money won't buy happiness, it will buy things that can go a long way toward making us happy. Ever thought about that? Now since we don't exactly have a lot of money (you don't really think we were paid a lot for this book, do you?), we think we would like to do some firsthand research in this area. If any of you have some extra money you would be willing to donate to our research project, please contact the publisher and find out how to get in touch with us. We sure would like to test our theory. (Don't do it! Really. We just wanted to see if you're paying very close attention to everything we say.)

**125**

*Get Wise! Mastering Vocabulary Skills*                    *www.petersons.com*

**What is all of this complaining about? Somebody got paid, and it wasn't me! *I* get nothing, nada, zip, zilch, zero!**

**benevolent** (adjective) wishing or doing good. *They may be the richest family in town, but they are also the most **benevolent**; they sponsor countless charities every year.*

**consummate** (verb) to complete, finish, or perfect. *He made his millions by working hard and being honest. He **consummates** every deal with a handshake.*

**covet** (verb) to be envious or jealous. *I try not to **covet** their beautiful Corvette, but it is such an incredible car!*

**eclectic** (adjective) drawn from many sources; varied, heterogeneous. *They have an **eclectic** portfolio with stock in such things as a toilet paper company, a children's TV show, and a flip-flop manufacturing company.*

**genial** (adjective) friendly, gracious. *Those kids are always so **genial**, you would never know their parents are multimillionaires.*

**opulent** (adjective) rich, lavish. *Their house is so **opulent** that it's hard to believe they would allow their gardener to shape their hedges into animal shapes.*

**philanthropist** (noun) one who gives freely.

They say he is a great **philanthropist**. Do you think he'd give a few bucks to a starving author?

**pompous** (adjective) arrogant. *You would think someone with that much money would be **pompous**, but he is really down to earth.*

**reciprocate** (verb) to make a return for something. *She always stresses the importance of **reciprocating** favors twofold.*

**usury** (noun) lending money at interest. *Many families make a lot of money through **usury**. I contribute quite a bit to the fortunes of those families!*

Do you ever think about what you would do with the cash if you were to win the lottery? Don't forget to save a lot of that money for Uncle Sam. Here's something else to think about. If you did win the lottery, would you become a philanthropist and share with your favorite author? Please?

## Get Wise!

Match each vocab word with its antonym.

1. _____ benevolent          A. shabby

2. _____ consummate          B. homogenous

3. _____ covet               C. humble

4. _____ eclectic            D. rude

5. _____ genial              E. greedy

6. _____ opulent             F. give away

7. _____ philanthropist      G. fail to finish

8. _____ pompous             H. keep

9. _____ reciprocate         I. miser

10. _____ usury              J. despise

## How Wise?

1. E; 2. G; 3. J; 4. B; 5. D; 6. A; 7. I; 8. C; 9. H; 10. F

# chapter 29

## It's Probably Wise to Avoid Children's TV

For whatever reason, some of you may really be able to relate to the things we're about to share with you. Whether or not you've got a little brother or sister running around the house, if you have seen even a few minutes of the popular children's TV shows, then you will know exactly what we're talking about and you will feel our pain. One of the countless things that change with the addition of a new child in the house is the nature of TV that is viewed in the house. We had always heard about those bizarre alien babies, that big purple dinosaur, the red dog, the blue dog, the turtle, and more. However, we had no idea of the far-reaching and long-lasting effects of these creatures. First, it's kind of spooky to see how a small child becomes en-tranced while watching these shows. Second, the cable channels play the same episodes over and over and over again. Finally, and most seriously, those darn jingles get stuck in your head the way bad songs do and they

**129**

*Get Wise! Mastering Vocabulary Skills*                    *www.petersons.com*

drive you crazy all day. If you don't believe us, just try watching those shows some time! In case you haven't been infected by these shows yet, here are some words of warning:

**What could be more fun than big, goofy, strangely colored creatures encouraging everyone to hug everyone else and always wear a smile? Well, come to think of it, that does sound kind of strange.**

**ambivalent** (adjective) having two or more contradictory feelings or attitudes; uncertain. *The characters on those kids' shows are always **ambivalent** and whiny about things. They want to eat, then they don't want to eat, then they do, and then they don't.*

**consolation** (noun) relief or comfort in sorrow or suffering.

Somebody on those shows always gets upset and needs **consolation**. The remedy is always a big hug and a cheesy grin.

**enmity** (noun) hatred, hostility, ill will. *Once those awful songs get stuck in your head and you walk around all day humming the theme song for the dinosaur show, you really start to develop some **enmity** toward that big stuffed character.*

**inevitable** (adjective) unable to be avoided. *With every one of these shows, it's **inevitable** that kids sing and dance and hug each other for the entire show.*

**mercurial** (adjective) changing quickly and unpredictably. *Those darn little dragons are so* **mercurial** *that you never know if they're going to laugh or cry, sing, or throw a tantrum.*

**mundane** (adjective) everyday, ordinary, commonplace. *It's disturbing to think that talking dinosaurs, babbling alien babies, giant red dogs, and goofy dragons can become so* **mundane** *so quickly.*

**placate** (verb) to soothe or appease by granting concessions. *You can bet that when those whiny little characters pitch a fit, someone will come along and* **placate** *them with some ridiculous thing like a flower or a sunbeam.*

**terrestrial** (adjective) of the Earth. *Sometimes I think that some non-* **terrestrial** *beings possess little kids who watch these shows and do some type of brainwashing to the kids.*

**turpitude** (noun) wickedness or depravity. *I think if one of the kids on that show with the purple dinosaur showed just a little* **turpitude***, it would really spice things up and make things more interesting.*

**winsome** (adjective) sweet and charming. *It would be one thing if those strange little characters were just* **winsome***, but they are so over the top with all the singing and dancing and hugging and smiling and . . . aaaahhhhh!!!!*

La la la, la la la, la la la la la la la la. You get the idea. To make matters worse, some very clever marketing executives put these annoying characters on everything from toothpaste to underwear to video games. You can't get away from them. They're everywhere!

Stop the insanity! AAAAHHHHH!!!!!

# Get Wise!

In each of the following sentences, fill in the blank with the correct vocab word.

**1.** If your little brother is driving you up the wall, just put in a videotape to _____ him and he'll be out of your hair for hours.

**2.** Imagine if there was just a little _____ between all those puppets on "Sesame Street"—what great TV that would be.

**3.** Those _____ little alien baby things can be happy, scared, excited, and sad all within a minute.

**4.** I must admit that I do find that cute little construction guy rather _____; there's just something kind of cute about him. Wait, what am I saying?

**5.** I am rather _____ about whether adults or kids actually write the scripts for the ridiculous shows.

**6.** I guess the producers are afraid that any _____ mixed into the shows might cause kids to grow up to be punks or something like that.

**7.** No matter how hard we may try to keep kids from finding these shows on TV, it is _____ that they will find the shows and that they will pitch a fit until we let them watch the shows.

**8.** Of all the children's characters that are popular these days, only a very few of them are _____ creatures that a kid might really see somewhere else besides on TV.

**9.** At least the bizarre little creatures on TV keep the kids entertained and prevent _____ Saturday mornings.

**10.** Well, if it's any _____, we probably drove our parents and siblings crazy with the things we watched, so maybe today's rug rats will turn out OK.

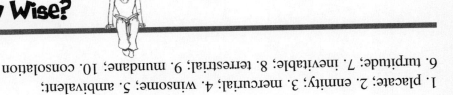

## How Wise?

1. placate; 2. enmity; 3. mercurial; 4. winsome; 5. ambivalent; 6. turpitude; 7. inevitable; 8. terrestrial; 9. mundane; 10. consolation

# chapter 30

# You're Wiser than Practically Everybody Else If You Know These Words

Earlier in the book, we looked at some words that are pretty obscure. Even though you may not use those words in everyday reading, writing, and speaking, the words may show up on a test at some point. Well, those words are *cat, dog,* and *ball* compared with the words we'll look at in this chapter. You may be wondering who the little old lady is out there who sits around and makes up these words. Well, we often wonder the same thing. If we ever find her, we'll let everyone else know where to find her, too, so we can ask her where she comes up with these crazy words. You know, when is the last time you heard someone using these words? By the way, don't even pretend like you already know what any of these words mean before you look at the definitions. Buckle up because these are going to be tricky:

They weren't kidding. These are some strange words. I don't think I have ever heard anyone using these before. I bet that know-it-all geek in your English class doesn't even know these.

**agathism** (noun) belief that things will work out for the good. *The cheerleader's* **agathism** *made us laugh out loud when she said that since the football season was canceled, the fans could pay more attention to the cheering on Friday nights.*

**caducity** (noun) infirmity or feebleness caused by old age. *One would think that Ozzy Osbourne would be aware of his own* **caducity***, but he just keeps on rockin'.*

**euthenics** (noun) making life better by improving the environment. *College guys practice* **euthenics** *by hanging posters and calendars of models in their rooms.*

**froward** (adjective) disobedient. *Most kids who are that* **froward** *are expelled by now, but he seems to have the principal wrapped around his finger.*

**ineluctable** (adjective) unavoidable. *I knew that being grounded was* **ineluctable** *when I broke the fish tank and the water from it destroyed not only my mother's 200-year-old Persian rug but also the antique hardwood floors underneath the rug.*

**melange** (noun) a strange mixture or combination. *The cheerleading sponsor's new "clique quota" placed a bizarre* **melange** *of geeks, jocks, preps, metalheads, and others on the squad.*

**obstreperous** (adjective) defiant.

My dog's **obstreperous** behavior drives me up the wall; he won't sit, speak, or roll over. The dog just sits there and looks at me defiantly.

**parvenu** (noun) the *nouveau riche* who have money but no status or power. *The well-established community thought of her as a* **parvenu** *when she won the lottery, then moved in on the wealthiest street in town.*

**tatterdemalion** (noun) someone who is always disheveled. *Bobcat Goldthwaite, that guy with a weird voice from the* Police Academy *movies, always looks like a* **tatterdemalion**.

**ukase** (noun) an edict or decree. *The president of the math club issued an* **ukase** *concerning the adoption of a new official calculator for the math club.*

You aren't fooling anyone by sitting there and smugly saying that you knew these. Heck, you don't even know if we're just making these up to fill these pages. Well, lucky for you, we wouldn't do that to you. All these words are real words, and you never know when one might pop up.

# Get Wise!

Match the vocab word with its synonym.

1. _____ agathism      **A.** inevitable

2. _____ caducity      **B.** antagonistic

3. _____ euthenics      **C.** order

4. _____ froward      **D.** heterogeneity

5. _____ ineluctable      **E.** frailty

6. _____ melange      **F.** having new wealth

7. _____ obstreperous      **G.** betterment

8. _____ parvenu      **H.** bum

9. _____ tatterdemalion      **I.** optimism

10. _____ ukase      **J.** contrary

# How Wise?

1. I; 2. E; 3. G; 4. J; 5. A; 6. D; 7. B; 8. F; 9. H; 10. C

# A Wise Person Also Knows the Lighter Side of History

History. Most people either love it or hate it. We guess it probably depends on whether a person's history teacher tells great stories or just requires the memorization of names, dates, places, and battles. Our history teachers in high school were pretty boring. In fact, we didn't even like history until we had a couple of great professors in college who turned us on to history. What we didn't realize was that history is full of strange, bizarre, and funny stories. We like to read and hear these stories because it reminds us that people are just weird. Although we'd like to tell you some funny stories, our job is to reveal some new words to you, so that's what we'll do. All these words have a place within the context of history, so keep these in mind the next time you want to score brownie points in history class:

My impression of a history teacher: "Read page 366. Define the bold words. Learn the dates. Test tomorrow." Sound familiar?

**abdicate** (verb) to give up a position of power. *Louis XVI never had a chance to* **abdicate** *his throne. He was arrested, tried, and then guillotined.*

**defenestration** (noun) throwing something from a window. *The Thirty Years War in Europe was started with the* **Defenestration** *of Prague. Basically, two Church officials were thrown out of a castle window. They survived because they landed in a dung heap.*

**diaspora** (noun) the exile of a people from their homeland. *Although they lost their homeland in the* **diaspora***, they eventually regained it hundreds of years later.*

**gerrymander** (verb) to redraw voting district lines so as to gain an advantage.

The word "**gerrymander**" is a combination of a guy's name and the word salamander. How'd you like to go down in history like that?

**interregnum** (noun) period of time between two kings or, more generally, governments. *King Ralph was actually a John Goodman film and not the king of the period in English history known as the "***interregnum***."*

**martyr** (noun) one who dies for a cause. *In the movie* Braveheart, *the English made a* **martyr** *of William Wallace and, instead of intimidating the Scots, inspired the Scots to win their independence from England.*

**muckraker** (verb) one who exposes political scandals. *Muckrakers have always had fun when people like "you-know-who" take office.*

**mugwump** (noun) a politician who is indecisive. *Nineteenth-century American politicians loved to use the term "mugwump" when talking about each other; today, politicians use words like, well, those four-letter ones.*

**theology** (noun) study of religion or God. *More wars have been fought over theology than over anything else. How ironic is that?*

**utopia** (noun) a perfect place. *In the 1500s, Thomas More wrote a book called Utopia about the perfect society; in Greek, utopia means "no place!"*

Have you heard some of these in history class before? Try this some time. Ask your teacher to tell you a good historical story. I promise it will liven things up a little in class.

 ## Get Wise!

Fill in the blank in each sentence with the correct vocab word.

1. With the way politicians behave today, a person could make a living as a _____.

2. The day that the biology students threw all the frogs out the window is now known around school as the "_____ of Frog."

3. The chess club experienced a tumultuous _____ between the resignation of the former president and the election of the new president.

4. In my opinion, _____ would be a place where summer is nine months long and school lasts only three months.

**5.** Is there any politician out there who isn't a _____? I just can't decide.

**6.** I sometimes feel a little sorry for a king who has to _____ his throne because I think it would be really cool to be a king.

**7.** There was a _____, of sorts, when the stink-bomb went off in the computer lab.

**8.** Joe gave up his wild and crazy bachelor life to settle down and study _____.

**9.** When the construction workers tried to knock down the oak tree to make a parking lot, the crazy environmentalist chained herself to the tree in an attempt to be a _____.

**10.** Some families in Arkansas are so big that politicians try to _____ the districts so that their whole families constitute a voting district.

# How Wise?

1. muckraker; 2. defenestration; 3. interregnum; 4. utopia; 5. mugwump; 6. abdicate; 7. diaspora; 8. theology; 9. martyr; 10. gerrymander

# chapter 32

# O Wise One

OK. Obviously, or not so obviously, we are going to observe some outrageous new words that all have one thing in common. Just from a quick observation, can you see anything out of the ordinary? Oh, come on.

Of course, there are way too many words that start with O in the sentences above. Cheesy way to make a point, we know, but the point is made and you won't forget it. There are several really good vocab words that start with O that we haven't already covered, and we are going to look at them in this chapter. Grouping them like this should really help you remember the words. This grouping will also help when you are trying to learn your flashcards. You are still using the flashcards, right? Good. Here are ten more words to add to your flashcard collection:

**Which is bigger, your flashcard collection or your little brother's baseball card collection?**

**objective** (adjective) dealing with observable facts rather than opinions or interpretations. *I need an* **objective** *opinion so I asked someone who doesn't care one way or the other—my little sister.*

**oblivious** (adjective) completely unaware. *The cheerleaders were completely* **oblivious** *to the fact that the team was in the locker room while they were still chanting D-E-F-E-N-S-E.*

**obscure** (adjective) little known; hard to understand. *Every time that teacher gives a bonus on a test, the question is about something so* **obscure** *that only a genius could answer the question.*

**obsequious** (adjective) subservient and servile. *The community service required by the school is to help foster an* **obsequious** *attitude and not for punishment, as many students think.*

**obsolescence** (noun) being antiquated or out of date. *Ever notice how electronics reach a state of* **obsolescence** *as soon as the warranty expires?*

**obtrusive** (adjective) overly prominent.

The geometry teacher has this big, **obtrusive**, hairy wart on the tip of her nose. In fact, she might be the Wicked Witch of the West!

**officious** (adjective) meddlesome. *I appreciated the tutor's help at first, but then she became* **officious** *and wanted to correct every single sentence I wrote.*

**omnipotent** (adjective) all-powerful. *Our school custodian thinks he is* **omnipotent** *because he has a key to all our lockers and all the teachers' rooms.*

**omniscient** (adjective) all-knowing. *Does it ever seem like your parents are* **omniscient**? *My parents always seemed to know every single thing I ever did.*

**onerous** (adjective) heavy, burdensome. *The assignment seemed quite* **onerous** *at first, but then, after I got a tutor who specialized in the subject, the assignment suddenly seemed easier.*

Obviously an outstanding collection of O words! I think these words are enough to make the average person say, "Oh yeah! Oh baby! Oh my gosh!" If you forget these words, you might be saying "Oh no" when you get to the SAT or whatever test you will be taking!

# Get Wise!

The underlined vocab words in the sentences below are in the *wrong* sentences. In the blank that follows each sentence, write the *correct* vocab word for that sentence.

1. When I score a touchdown to win the game for my team, I actually feel <u>obtrusive</u>. _____

---

**2.** Strangely enough, most famous people come from some <u>omnipotent</u> little place with a small population. _____

**3.** We all think the calculus teacher reached the point of <u>oblivious</u> about thirty years ago. _____

**4.** Sometimes parents can become <u>obsolescence</u> even though they are just trying to help. _____

**5.** Pulling the gum off the bottoms of all the desks in school was quite an <u>objective</u> task, but that's what we got for blowing a bubble and putting it in the cheerleader's hair. _____

**6.** It is almost impossible to be <u>officious</u> when judging a beauty pageant when your girlfriend is a contestant. _____

**7.** The new billboard was so <u>omniscient</u> that the city took the sign down. Did they even consider that it said, "Welcome to our city"?

_____

**8.** My girlfriend said she would never be so <u>onerous</u> as to pull my shoes off and rub my feet. _____

**9.** I slept so hard in class the other day that I was <u>obsequious</u> to the fact that the bell rang and my class left for lunch. _____

**10.** He must be <u>obscure</u> because he has never missed a single question on a test or assignment in his entire high school career.

_____

## How Wise?

1. omnipotent; 2. obscure; 3. obsolescence; 4. officious; 5. onerous; 6. objective; 7. obtrusive; 8. obsequious; 9. oblivious; 10. omniscient

# Puzzle 5

Complete the following puzzle using the words you just learned in this chapter. Puzzle solutions are in the back of the book.

## Across

7. unavoidable
9. religion
11. decree
12. hatred
14. soothe
16. little-known
17. detect
18. perfect place
19. prominent

## Down

1. endanger
2. in secret
3. meddlesome
4. burdensome
5. commonplace
6. unaware
8. disobedient
9. uncertain
10. admire
13. estrange
15. frailty

# A Wise Person Knows: Too
# Risqué or Not Risqué

Have you ever heard someone say something and then you thought, "Oh my gosh! I can't believe she just said that in front of everyone. Wait a minute, I don't even know what that means, anyway. Can she really say that?" The point we're trying to make here is that there are some words you just know are lewd or just plain inappropriate. Some words refer to something obscene, but the words themselves are actually OK to say or write. Then there are some words that sound inappropriate but actually have a very innocent meaning. Those are the best words. If you say those in public, people will give you some very strange looks. Learn these words and then try them out in public.

Before we look at all the definitions, let's see the list of words we are going to work with in this chapter. Be warned, a few of these words have a

149

*Get Wise! Mastering Vocabulary Skills*                    www.petersons.com

risqué meaning, but most are very innocent. See if you know which are which. Here's the list: castigate, amorous, masticate, bailiwick, circumambulate, boondoggle, lissome, titular, oscillate, osculate:

**OK, close the door before you get started learning *this* list. Ha, ha. I hate to disappoint you, but most of these just *sound* risqué. Let's take a closer look.**

**amorous** (adjective) indicative of love. *It's not uncommon for him to send* **amorous** *glances her way during homeroom.*

**bailiwick** (noun) province, domain, or jurisdiction. *The jester said to the king, "We had no idea that the* **bailiwick** *was so vast."*

**boondoggle** (noun) impasse or deadlock. *The two lovebirds were in the midst of quite a* **boondoggle** *when they both realized how silly they were being.*

**castigate** (verb) reprimand, rebuke. *Their parents like to* **castigate** *their naughty kids whenever they can; they're always so critical of those two.*

**circumambulate (verb) to walk around.**

She **circumambulated** the entire football team before she chose her date for the homecoming dance.

**lissome** (adjective) supple, agile, athletic. *He wanted a* **lissome** *date for the dance, so he started asking girls from the basketball team.*

**masticate** (verb) chew. *Always* **masticate** *your food twenty times.*

---

**oscillate** (verb) swing or turn. *How did that huge pyramid of cheerleaders* **oscillate** *like that in front of the entire student body?*

**osculate** (verb) kiss. *It is against the rules at our school to* **osculate** *in the halls.*

**titular** (adjective) in name only. *She was the* **titular** *queen of the school, but no one else thought that.*

What can we say? Those are just some *interesting* words. Just remember that you better know what they mean before you start throwing them around at the dinner table.

# Get Wise!

Match the vocab word with its synonym.

1. _____ bailiwick
2. _____ boondoggle
3. _____ castigate
4. _____ circumambulate
5. _____ oscillate
6. _____ amorous
7. _____ lissome
8. _____ masticate
9. _____ osculate
10. _____ titular

A. criticize
B. flexible
C. oscillate
D. kiss
E. region
F. self-titled
G. in love
H. munch
I. encircle
J. stalemate

# How Wise?

1. E; 2. J; 3. A; 4. I; 5. C; 6. G; 7. B; 8. H; 9. D; 10. F

# Choose Wisely When Buying a Used Car

Ah, the very first car. We remember it so vividly. Have you ever seen a completely gutted, pale blue 1970-something Ford? No air conditioning, no stereo, a standard transmission, with the shifter behind the steering wheel and ugly wheels and tires. Not exactly the cool boy or girl magnet, right? It was ugly and so not cool. You see, the parents who thought they were getting a great deal got conned big time! Here's some good advice for all of you who'll be driving in the next few years, if you aren't already: Be careful, be *very* careful when you get to buy your first car, especially if it's a used car! The trick is not to get it *too* used!

**153**

*Get Wise! Mastering Vocabulary Skills*                    *www.petersons.com*

**My first car is going to be sooo cool. In fact, I've already picked it out. The trick is trying to figure out how I'm going to pay for it!**

**anachronistic** (adjective) out of the proper time. *When you pick out a car, make sure it isn't too* **anachronistic**. *You don't want to try to maintain a car that your great, great grandfather might have driven!*

**encroach** (verb) to go beyond acceptable limits; to trespass. *Be careful not to allow the car salesperson to* **encroach** *on any conversations you and your parents have about your new car; they are notorious for trying to "make you a great deal on that little marvel."*

**esculent** (adjective) edible. *Don't let the car salesperson try to sell you those* **esculent** *air fresheners! They taste worse than they smell!*

**florid** (adjective) flowery, fancy; reddish. *Don't let that car salesperson convince you that a rusty car just has "a delicate* **florid** *tone."*

**irrational** (adjective) unreasonable. *Most importantly, don't get* **irrational** *about the purchase and allow the salesperson to sell you a Gremlin, a Pacer, or a K Car!*

**nondescript** (adjective) without distinctive qualities; drab. *It may not be so bad to settle for a* **nondescript** *car; you must admit that your car is less likely to get stolen if it isn't very attractive.*

**pallid (adjective) pale; dull.**

One thing is for sure, a **pallid** color on your car gets you one step closer to convincing your parents to get you a sweet new paint job.

**plastic** (adjective) able to be molded or reshaped. *Make sure you aren't buying a car whose major parts are* **plastic** *and easily bent, shaped, or molded.*

**tenebrous** (adjective) dark and gloomy. *If you are into the gothic scene, maybe you should consider a* **tenebrous** *looking car with gray or black paint and dark-tinted windows.*

**translucent** (adjective) letting some light pass through. *If you decide to get your windows tinted, you have to keep them somewhat* **translucent**—*unless, of course, you are a vampire in which case you might want them just painted black!*

Just take this book with you when you and your parents head down to that used-car lot to pick out your ride. Above all, make sure you don't buy from any car lot whose name begins with "Honest." You know, like "Honest Abe's Autos" or "Honest Rod's Cool Rides."

# Get Wise!

Match each of the following vocab words with its antonym.

1. _____ anachronistic     **A. ornamental**

2. _____ encroach     **B. timely**

3. _____ esculent     **C. bright**

4. _____ florid     **D. cheery**

5. _____ irrational     **E. malleable**

6. _____ nondescript     **F. logical**

7. _____ pallid     **G. clear**

8. _____ plastic     **H. retreat**

9. _____ tenebrous     **I. interesting**

10. _____ translucent     **J. inedible**

# How Wise?

1. E; 2. J; 3. A; 4. I; 5. C; 6. G; 7. B; 8. H; 9. D; 10. F

# Choose Wisely When Choosing Your Coffee

Are you a coffee drinker? How about espresso? Cappuccino? We like all kinds. Some of us really like those trendy designer coffees that cost about $4 or $5 per cup. I know that's crazy, but we can't help it. What's really crazy is all those ingredients that these places have to add to their coffees. "I'd like an extra grande latte with a drip of caramel laced with cinnamon, and I'd like a squirt of milk topped off with crème and hazelnut sprinkles." We even saw one place that had about thirty different toppings, syrups, and other things for their coffee. All the names that these coffee companies have for their drinks are pretty boring. So we've come up with some pretty good ones, and we're going to share them with you. By the way, did we mention the vocab that's included in the names?

**157**

*Get Wise! Mastering Vocabulary Skills*  www.petersons.com

What's wrong with that simple black coffee that my grandpa used to make?

**coalesce** (verb) to come together. *The "Coffee Coalescence"—The perfect combination of coffee, cappuccino, and espresso to wake you up in the morning.*

**composure** (noun) calm, self-assurance. *The "Lose Your Composure Latte"—Double the caffeine means you can't ever be calm!*

**derivative** (adjective) taken from a particular source. *The "Doughnut Derivative Decaf"—For the mornings when you don't have time to eat, this beverage has all the goodness of ground-up doughnuts mixed right into your coffee.*

**eminent** (adjective) noteworthy, famous. *The "Eminent Espresso"—Simply the best, and soon to be the most famous, espresso on the market.*

**enigma** (noun) a baffling situation. *The "Enigma Espresso"—There is something interesting about this baffling beverage, but we can't quite figure out what it is.*

**ephemeral** (adjective) quickly disappearing; transient. *The "Ephemeral Espresso"—If you're in a real hurry, this elusive espresso is gone before you know it!*

**interminable** (adjective) endless or seemingly endless. *The "Interminable au Lait"—This bottomless beverage is for the coffee drinker who never wants the experience to end.*

**languid** (adjective) without energy; slow, sluggish, listless. *The "Languid Latte"—The decaffeinated latte for those who love the coffee but hate the caffeine.*

**penitent** (adjective) feeling sorry for past crimes or sins.

The "**Penitent** Pint"—The pint of plain, black coffee to have the day after you've been really bad and have had one of those extra-large, high-fat, high-calorie cappuccinos.

**temerarious** (adjective) reckless and daring. *The "Tall **Temerarious** One"—The tall coffee carelessly created by randomly adding a sampling of bold ingredients; who knows what you'll get?*

# Get Wise!

Circle the word in each of the following word groups that does not belong.

1. coalesce     unite     disjoin     fuse

2. impatience     calm     equanimity     composure

3. offshoot     cause     derivative     by-product

4. celebrated     eminent     obscure     exalted

5. enigma     puzzle     riddle     explanation

6. permanent     fleeting     short-lived     ephemeral

7. continual     interminable     eternal     ceasing

8. weary     energetic     languid     exhausted

9. remorseful     boastful     sorry     penitent

10. free     temerarious     bold     reserved

# How Wise?

1. disjoin; 2. impatience; 3. cause; 4. obscure; 5. explanation; 6. permanent; 7. ceasing; 8. energetic; 9. boastful; 10. reserved.

# Movies You'd Be Wise Not to See

We don't know about you, but we love to watch movies. We like all kinds of movies—action, comedy, adventure, drama, sports, romance (don't tell anybody, though), and even old black-and-white movies. We guess you could say that movie-watching is one of our hobbies. We have seen so many movies that we now consider ourselves movie experts. There are so many fantastic movies out there, movies like *Braveheart, The Matrix, Remember the Titans,* and *Casablanca.* On the other hand, there are some really horrible movies, too, like *Ishtar, Fair Game,* and *Freddy Got Fingered.* At this point, movies are so numerous that it would be wise to pick and choose very care-

**161**

*Get Wise! Mastering Vocabulary Skills*                    *www.petersons.com*

fully the movies you see. Nothing frustrates us more than spending 2 hours and a lot of money watching an awful movie. Speaking of awful movies, you'll find a few movies in our definitions to avoid at all costs:

**Instead of playing "Six Degrees of Kevin Bacon," maybe you should try playing "Six Degrees of Chi."**

**decimate** (verb) to destroy. The Dog that Ate Dallas *is a movie about a giant Chihuahua that* **decimates** *downtown Dallas. I give it a big thumbs down!*

**conflagration** (noun) a devastating fire. The California **Conflagration** *is about a boy scout campfire that burns out of control and eventually destroys the entire state of California.*

**invincible** (adjective) impossible to conquer or overcome. Ira the **Invincible** *chronicles the life of Ira Messenberger, the undefeated Romanian Ping-Pong champion.*

**mercenary** (noun) a hired fighter. I Clash for Cash *is a terrible movie about a guy during the Great Depression who tries to find work as a* **mercenary** *when he loses his factory job.*

**miasma** (noun) toxic swamp vapor. *The worst movie of all-time has to be* The **Miasma** of Miami, *a flick about a gaseous monster that suffocates the entire city of Miami.*

**nomad (noun) one who wanders in search of food.**

The **Nomad** is a documentary about an aboriginal Australian who travels the outback in search of lunch.

**obliterate** (verb) to wipe out or destroy. The Ostrich that **Obliterated** Omaha *is a low-budget flick about a zoological experiment gone bad that results in a giant ostrich strutting around in Nebraska destroying everything in its path.*

**permeate** (verb) to seep through. The Incredible Oozing Stuff *is another low-budget movie. This one is about some goo that* **permeates** *the earth's crust and dissolves both cities and citydwellers.*

**sloth** (noun) laziness; one who is lazy. *I left halfway through* My Life as a **Sloth**, *a movie about a guy who spends three straight years sitting on his couch watching TV.*

**tryst** (noun) secret meeting of lovers. The **Tryst** in the Mist *is an experimental film about two lovers who meet in a park in London. The problem with the movie is that the fog is so thick you can't see the characters throughout the entire movie!*

The only reason you should ever see any of these films is if you are having serious bouts of insomnia. These movies will remedy even the worst cases of sleeplessness. They would also be good for a laugh or two, especially the ones that are supposed to be scary.

Do you think anyone will ever make this book into a movie? Nope, neither do I, but the author got the rights!

# Get Wise!

Fill in the blank in each sentence with the correct vocab word.

1. Named for its slowness and sluggishness, the _____ is a very strange and unusual animal.

**2.** A swamp often produces a _____ of methane gas because of all the waste products in the soil there.

**3.** The archaeologist studied the site of the _____ because the charred remains actually offered a great deal of historical evidence.

**4.** The cheerleader and the chess club treasurer met behind the bleachers for a _____ because nobody would have accepted the relationship if it were made public.

**5.** An epidemic of mono could _____ the cheerleading squad for the entire football season. Oh, well.

**6.** When I think of a _____, I think of a caveman who is wandering around with a club looking for a saber-toothed tiger to whack on the head and eat.

**7.** If this book doesn't sell, I may enlist as a _____ in the army of some Central American country.

**8.** I would _____ the hard drive if I were to trip and drop the computer.

**9.** When Michael Jordan was in his prime, his team was practically _____.

**10.** The smell of the cafeteria can somehow _____ every wall in the school and make everyone sick by mid-morning.

# How Wise?

1. sloth; 2. miasma; 3. conflagration; 4. tryst; 5. decimate; 6. nomad; 7. mercenary; 8. obliterate; 9. invincible; 10. permeate

# The First Annual Wise Awards

You have probably noticed that there are more award shows today than ever before. We have always had the Oscars, the Emmys, the Grammys, the Tonys, and a few others. Then, a few years ago, others jumped on the bus: Blockbuster, Nickelodeon, ESPN, and MTV got into the act by creating their own awards. Now it seems like everyone has its own awards. Well, they say if you can't beat them, join them. So, we have created our Wise awards to dish out to famous, celebrated, and those notorious people from various walks of life. Legally, we have to inform you that the selection process was carefully monitored by the accounting firm of Dewey, Cheatum, and Howe (very old joke...think Three Stooges), and all decisions are final. And now, the moment you've all been waiting for...

**165**

*Get Wise! Mastering Vocabulary Skills*                    www.petersons.com

Oooh. Just found out I've been nominated for six awards. My fans think I'll win at least three. I've been working so hard on my acceptance speech. Wait until you hear all of those big words I've been picking up along the way.

**bellwether** (noun) one who takes leadership of something. *Britney Spears wins this year's "Bad Fashion **Bellwether**" award for her wardrobe.*

**claque** (noun) an audience that is paid for applause. *My cousin gets the "**Claque** of the Year" Award for setting the record for attending more talk-show tapings than anyone else in history. He actually got paid to sit in the studio audience for Howie Mandel's show, Arsenio Hall's show, and numerous other shows that were just plain awful!*

**depreciate** (verb) to decrease in value.

Have you seen that show *American Idol*? I'm sure Simon's harsh critiques of some of the contestants will **depreciate** in value once they start making millions of dollars.

**destitute** (adjective) extremely poor. *This year's winner of the "Depreciate Your Company's Value to the Point that Your Employees will all be **Destitute**" award is (and the decision was unanimous) none other than Endrun.*

**edacious** (adjective) having a voracious and insatiable appetite. *The winner of the "Most Audacious, Voracious, and **Edacious**" award goes to that funny, swollen character that Martin Short plays on his TV show.*

**fluke** (noun) an event that happens by luck. *The "**Fluke** of the Year" award has to go to the New England Patriots for their unlikely win in the Super Bowl.*

**iconoclast** (noun) someone who attacks traditional beliefs or institutions. *This year's "**Iconoclast** of the Year" award goes to the guy everybody loves to be afraid of, Marilyn Manson.*

**indubitable** (adjective) unquestionable. *The **indubitable** winner of the "Idiot of the Year" goes to Tom Cruise for not staying with Nicole Kidman—she's hot!*

**inveterate** (adjective) persistent, habitual. *For his **inveterate** behavior, Homer Simpson is this year's recipient of the "Here We Go Again" award.*

**resilient** (adjective) able to recover from difficulty. *The "Comeback Person of the Year" award goes to Michael Jordan for being more **resilient** than anyone thought he could be. Jordan is also in the running for the "Tough Break" award.*

Each of this year's recipients was unable to be here for one reason or another. In addition, all refused to comment or to send an acceptance speech. In fact, we don't even have the addresses to send the awards to the winners. We're not really sure what we're going to do with all these nifty little trophies. If nobody claims them, we guess we'll just give out twice as many next year. Oh, well.

# Get Wise!

The underlined vocab words in the sentences below are in the *wrong* sentences. In the blank that follows each sentence, write the *correct* vocab word for that sentence.

1. He was the <u>destitute</u> choice for class president because he was the only guy running who wasn't wearing coke-bottle glasses and a pocket protector. _____

2. The value of my baseball cards will almost certainly <u>claque</u> if they ever got rained on._____

**3.** She was the <u>fluke</u> of the movement to get reserved parking for freshmen. She was also the only freshman who drove a car.
_____

**4.** Years ago, a basketball player who wore long shorts was considered an <u>edacious</u>. _____

**5.** The team was very <u>indubitable</u>; after being down fifty in the first half, the team lost by only one point in triple overtime.
_____

**6.** My dog is the most <u>iconoclast</u> animal I have ever seen; it ate our entire Thanksgiving dinner when we were in the living room.
_____

**7.** It was just a <u>bellwether</u> that he passed that test because he made little patterns with his answer sheet. _____

**8.** His <u>depreciate</u> coffee drinking makes him so jumpy and edgy that he could easily bounce off the walls. _____

**9.** The stand-up comedian got into trouble with the IRS when he tried to claim several payments to an entire professional <u>inveterate</u> as a tax write-off. _____

**10.** I always wonder how former athletes and other celebrities can be filthy rich one year and then be <u>resilient</u> the next. _____

## How Wise?

1. indubitable; 2. depreciate; 3. bellwether; 4. iconoclast; 5. resilient; 6. edacious; 7. fluke; 8. inveterate; 9. claque; 10. destitute

# Puzzle 7

Complete the following puzzle using the words you just learned in this chapter. Puzzle solutions are in the back of the book.

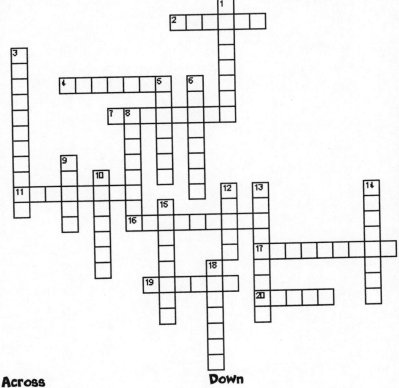

**Across**

2. vapor
4. supple
7. destroy
11. seep through
16. dark
17. mistress
19. pale
20. lovers' meeting

**Down**

1. kiss
3. drab
5. famous
6. unite
8. edible
9. wanderer
10. sluggish
12. laziness
13. criticize
14. sorry
15. trespass
18. self-titled

# A Fashion-Wise Person Knows What's Fashionable and What's Not

If you are like 99.9 percent of all other hip American kids, you are at least somewhat interested in and concerned about fashion trends. Does that mean you keep up with all the trends by wearing all the newest styles or that you speak using all the latest slang? Of course not, but you are almost certainly aware of them. Even if you are the fraction of a percent of the population that chooses to be totally individualistic with your dress, you know what's "groovy" and "far out" and "neat" and "hip" and "phat." Have you noticed how the language changes as much as the fashion? Who in the world says

**171**

*Get Wise! Mastering Vocabulary Skills*                    *www.petersons.com*

"phat" anymore? Let's take a few moments to drive down memory lane (did you get that new car yet?) and take a look at some of the more interesting trends of the recent decades. Yeah, we know that most of you only know about some of these trends because you've seen them on TV. Lucky you—we lived through some of it!

Did I miss the chapter with *groovy* in it? What is that?

**abysmal** (adjective) wretched. *During the 1980s, rock bands often wore those* **abysmal** *tight vinyl pants.*

**augment** (verb) increase, enlarge. *In the last twenty years, it has become quite fashionable to* **augment** *one's body parts; that's all I have to say about that subject.*

**eccentric** (adjective) unconventional. *Thankfully, Elton John and his* **eccentric** *fashion sense have never had much of an influence on the fashion of the nation's youth.*

**flagrant** (adjective) obviously wrong; offensive. *During the 1980s, the* **flagrant** *use of neon colors and big hair was commonplace.*

**guileless** (adjective) without cunning; innocent. *When I see old pictures, I always feel bad for the* **guileless** *children whose fashionably challenged parents dressed them in plaid bell-bottoms, a brown shirt, knee-high tube socks, and Converse All-Star sneakers.*

**manifest** (verb) to exhibit or show. *The grunge music scene of Seattle did* **manifest** *itself in fashion when everyone started wearing flannel shirts.*

**mimicry** (noun) imitation, aping. *Sadly,* **mimicry** *of celebrities often leads to widespread bad fashion. For example, thousands of teenage girls wore really bad outfits after Madonna burst onto the scene.*

**mutable** (adjective) likely to change. *Thankfully, because most of the hairstyles that are popular on TV are rather mutable, bad hair trends don't last as long as other trends do.*

**palatable** (adjective) pleasant or agreeable. *The fashions of the 1950s are palatable only if you are a big fan of either* Grease *or* Leave It to Beaver.

**stymie (verb) hinder or block.**

A lack of money will **stymie** your fashion statements if you don't know how to shop wisely.

Why does it seem that every ten years or so, we all look back and say what horrible fashions we had in the previous decade? You just wait, one day you'll look at your high school pictures and think, "How could I have been so stupid? What was I wearing? What was I *thinking*?" We promise that you *will* feel that way. Oops, we hope we haven't ruined the next ten years for you, but it's only the truth. Sorry 'bout that.

## Get Wise!

Match the vocabulary word with its synonym.

1._____ abysmal      **A.** intentional

2._____ augment      **B.** changing

3._____ eccentric      **C.** display

4._____ flagrant      **D.** amplify

5._____ guileless      **E.** inhibit

6._____ manifest      **F.** delectable

7._____ mimicry      **G.** impersonation

8._____ mutable      **H.** odd

9._____ palatable      **I.** naive

10._____ stymie      **J.** awful

# How Wise?

1.J; 2.D; 3.H; 4.A; 5.I; 6.C; 7.G; 8.B; 9.F; 10.E

# It Would Be Wise Not to Take Yourself Too Seriously

One of the biggest mistakes that people make is taking themselves too seriously. People from all walks of life do this everyday. A lot of actors think that they are God's gift to the world. Some professional athletes think that the entire industry revolves around them. The worst, however, are those people who think they are the smartest and most important people in the entire free world. We see this everyday, and we're sure you do, too. You should learn a very important lesson from these folks. Don't take yourself so seriously. It will just lead to stress, lots of unnecessary stress. You know what we'd like to tell these people? "Have some fun! You don't really want to end up like that stuffy old codger we sent packing in the introduction, do you?"

**175**

*Get Wise! Mastering Vocabulary Skills*                    *www.petersons.com*

**These people obviously can't be serious very often. On the other hand, maybe they're always serious and this book is their outlet for all that bottled-up bad humor and those ridiculous one-liners.**

**bumptious** (adjective) conceited, arrogant. *Is it any wonder that **bumptious** people like him never have a girlfriend longer than 15 minutes?*

**decry** (verb) to criticize or condemn. *Movie critics who **decry** every movie they see are either just jealous that they don't look good enough to be in movies or bitter that they once got rejected at a movie audition.*

**delegate** (verb) to give authority or responsibility. *Don't you just despise people who always act like the only way things will get done right is if they do things themselves? They need to lighten up and **delegate** some authority every once in a while.*

**divination** (noun) the art of predicting the future. *Some of the funniest people on TV are the small-town TV station weathermen who act like they have the gift of **divination** but are wrong more often than they are right about the weather.*

**empirical** (adjective) based on experience or personal observation. *Based on the **empirical** evidence I've collected over the years, people who take themselves too seriously are always the butt of everybody else's jokes.*

**hierarchy** (noun) a ranking of people, things, or ideas from highest to lowest. *In the social **hierarchy** of most places, people who take themselves too seriously think they are at the top while everybody else thinks they are bottom-dwellers.*

**invariable** (adjective) unchanging, constant. *She always speaks in an **invariable** tone because she thinks she sounds more intelligent that way. She really should read the sentence for "hierarchy"!*

**mollify** (verb) to soothe or calm; to appease. *A person with a sense of humor can mollify others much easier than someone who's wound up too tight.*

**proximity** (noun) closeness, nearness. *The proximity of his mirrors to his bed, his kitchen table, his sofa, and his computer makes me think his favorite pastime is looking at himself and admiring his good looks.*

**servile** (adjective) like a slave or servant; submissive. *What is it with these rich people who think that everyone in lower tax brackets should have a servile attitude while in their presence? Get a grip, people!*

You know exactly the type of wingnuts we're talking about, don't you? Now we don't want to be too hard on those guys. We're sure there is some reason why they're like that. We won't even pretend to be psychologists (touchy subject!) and figure why they are the way they are but they are.

# Get Wise!

Match each vocab word with its antonym.

1. _____ bumptious          A. speculative

2. _____ decry              B. incite

3. _____ delegate           C. do-it-yourself

4. _____ divination         D. changing

5. _____ empirical          E. meek

6. _____ hierarchy          F. far away

7. _____ invariable         G. demanding

8. _____ mollify            H. anarchy

9. _____ proximity          I. build up

10. _____ servile           J. guess blindly

# How Wise?

1. E; 2. I; 3. C; 4. J; 5. A; 6. H; 7. D; 8. B; 9. F; 10. G

# chapter 40

# You Are the Wisest of the Wise if You Can Add these Words to Your Vocabulary

Can you believe that our little journey is almost over? We can't. In fact, we're starting to get all weepy. Excuse me while we grab a tissue. Just think, when you started this book you didn't know *bumptious* from *scrumptious*. Now you are a veritable vocab master. Well, almost. One more chapter and you will be. Now we have done two chapters that have some really crazy words, but we saved the best for next to last (that's much more original than "the best for last"). This chapter contains perhaps our favorite of all the really difficult, really bizarre words. I know you tried to pretend like you knew those other words, but you can't even pretend here. These are the most outlandish, most ridiculous, most insane words ever. I promise that if you use these in a paper or on a test, your teachers will mark them wrong be-

**479**

*Get Wise! Mastering Vocabulary Skills*                    *www.petersons.com*

cause they will think you made up these words all by yourself. Here they are—ten totally, completely useless but extremely testable words:

**Just when you thought they had run out of weird words, they've got even more up their sleeves. These authors must have the most brilliant minds of our time! Or maybe they really are crazy! Uh, oh . . .**

**arriviste** (noun) an upstart or one who moves up the social scale. *With the millions of dollars and the worldwide critical acclaim I get from this book, I will certainly be one of* Fortune *500's "Top 500* **Arrivistes***" for 2002!*

**bowdlerize** (verb) to rewrite in a rough or crude manner. *If my editor doesn't like my work, she might give it to her six-year-old to* **bowdlerize**.

**brummagem** (adjective) bogus, fake. *Perhaps one day I'll be exposed as* **brummagem** *and someone will realize that I am actually that old guy who was mentioned at the beginning of the book.*

**comestibles** (noun) something edible. *All this writing is making me quite hungry. I think I will go and search for* **comestibles** *in that dark, dank refrigerator of mine.*

**éclat** (noun) great success. *My editor said that I won't get paid if this book isn't regarded as an* **éclat***, so please write, call, and e-mail to tell my editor how much your life has been changed through my inspirational writings.*

**galoot** (noun) oaf. *That big galoot that I call a boss didn't even know that "* **galoot** *" was a word!*

**hugger-mugger** (noun) a big confused mess. *Hopefully his essay will be the best thing he's ever written and not just some big* **hugger-mugger** *that a crotchety old man scribbled in his spare time.*

**lachrymose** (adjective) mournful. *Did I mention how* **lachrymose** *I have become as we near the end of our journey together?*

**nabob (noun) an influential, affluent person.**

I have always wanted to be called a **nabob**, haven't you? Maybe this book is my ticket to nabobability (is that a word?).

**sciolism** (noun) superficial or trivial knowledge. *I hope you don't fall victim to* **sciolism** *but rather develop a deep comprehension and love of words the way that I have. I'm getting misty-eyed again.*

Ah! We love those words; don't you? You'll really love them when you see them on some test and you know exactly what they mean. Even if you don't see them on a test before you get into college, you may run into some of them while you're there. Hang on to those flashcards!

# Get Wise!

Fill in the blank with the correct vocab word.

1. When the computer virus attacked my hard drive, all that was left was a big _____.

2. Jordan's return to the NBA can't really be described as a big _____.

3. His _____ claims that he was abducted by aliens made everyone in school roll on the floor with laughter.

4. The inventor of the little yellow Post-It Notes must have been an _____ after everyone saw how great his invention was.

**5.** His class on "How to Win at Trivial Pursuit" unabashedly promotes
_____.

**6.** She became so _____ when her nail polish chipped that her mascara ran all over her face.

**7.** The big _____ picked up the football and stumbled sixty yards downfield toward the endzone.

**8.** Only stuffy people call food something as ridiculous as _____.

**9.** I once had a student _____ an encyclopedia article and turn it in as his own. Then he had the audacity to ask why his grade was so low!

**10.** Wouldn't it be weird if your name was Robert and you won the lottery and you were a really important person? Then people would say, "Hey! Rob the _____!"

# How Wise?

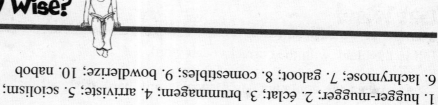

1. huger-mugger; 2. éclat; 3. brummagem; 4. arriviste; 5. sciolism; 6. lachrymose; 7. galoot; 8. comestibles; 9. bowdlerize; 10. nabob

# chapter 11

# Now, Don't You Feel Infinitely Wiser Than You Did at the Beginning of This Book?

Well, here we are at the end of our journey. It has been quite an adventure, full of incredible memories and beautiful Kodak moments. You know, there were times when . . . (pause for effect), we didn't know if we would make it. It makes us misty-eyed just thinking about how far you've come in the long, arduous hours that we've spent together. You started as just another potential Miss Malaprop, and now you are a word warrior ready to do verbal combat with any verbally challenged person who may come your way. Ah, how proud you have made us all. All of a sudden we feel a bout of empty-nest syndrome overtaking our very being. As Shakespeare would say, "Parting is such sweet sorrow." (Remember him? He was in Chapter 1.) This must be

**183**

*Get Wise! Mastering Vocabulary Skills*                    *www.petersons.com*

how parents feel when their oldest child takes that triumphant walk across the graduation stage. Oh boy, we can hear "Pomp and Circumstance" echoing in the background (you know, that song that the high school band plays at graduation every year and you always wondered what it was called). Listen closely, can you hear it, too? Is your chest swelling with pride the way ours is? What a beautiful moment! We wish this could last forever. Actually, we guess it can as long as you don't turn the page. Uh, it just dawned on us that we aren't quite finished yet. We still have one more vocab lesson! Nuts, all that beautiful eloquent language uttered prematurely. Oh, well. Until next time . . .

Enough of the melodrama, already! Can we leave with our pride at least a little intact?

**adulation** (noun) extreme admiration. *Right now, your friends should be offering you some much-deserved* **adulation** *for the incredible verbal strides you have made because of this book.*

**chaos** (noun) disorder, confusion, chance. *Now armed with hundreds of outstanding vocab words, you no longer have to live in verbal* **chaos** *like so many others (like the cheerleading squad).*

**engender** (verb) to produce, to cause. *Your completion of this book is certain to* **engender** *a sense of pride and satisfaction in all our hearts, second only to the time our editorial director's dog finished first at the local kennel club's dog show.*

**eradicate** (verb) to destroy completely. *It is our hope that this book has inspired you to devote the rest of your natural-born life to* **eradicating** *malapropisms wherever they may rear their ugly heads.*

**extricate** (verb) to free from a difficult or complicated situation. *Never again will teachers have to* **extricate** *good vocabulary words from your brain. Now your brain runneth over with great vocab!*

**intrepid** (adjective) fearless and resolute. *We wish you nothing but the best in your **intrepid** pursuit of a new life as a defender of the dictionary and a vanquisher of the verbally challenged.*

**laudatory** (adjective) giving praise. *I bet you can't wait for your friends, family, teachers, and strangers to start sending you **laudatory** messages.*

**persevere** (adjective) to continue despite difficulties. *Because you have **persevered** so long and hard, you are now ready to make your way into the harsh, cruel world known as high school armed only with your wits, this book, and your trusty flashcards.*

**unheralded** (adjective) little known, unexpected. *No longer will you have to live your life as an **unheralded** scholar; you are certain to emerge as the most verbose and loquacious person in your entire class.*

**venerate** (verb) to admire or honor. *As you head out into the world, just remember that the most important thing you can do with your new-and-improved vocab skills is to **venerate** the authors for their tireless efforts and witty, if not brilliant, charm.*

It's over already? I don't know about you, but I feel totally wise now. One question, though. Who's that Shakespeare guy they were talking about? Is he going to be on a test or something? Anyway, I'm out. Peace!

# Get Wise!

Fill in the blank with the correct word.

1.  The newspaper had some very _____ comments for the sold-out opening night performance.

2. Gardeners always try to _____ all the harmful insects in their gardens.

3. When the rat crawled into the school cafeteria, _____ erupted and it took hours to settle everyone down.

4. The rescue worker had to _____ the woman from the wreckage of the car.

5. It is important to _____ at a difficult task even if you have been unsuccessful in the past.

6. Great movies can _____ feelings of either happiness or sadness.

7. The Baseball Hall of Fame was established to _____ the greatest players of all time.

8. The small, intimate, _____ restaurants are often some of the best places to eat.

9. The audience showered the singer with _____ after the concert.

10. The chess club's _____ pursuit of perfection finally earned them a first-place finish in the annual chess tournament held in the library basement every year.

# How Wise?

1. laudatory; 2. eradicate; 3. chaos; 4. extricate; 5. persevere; 6. engender; 7. venerate; 8. unheralded; 9. adulation; 10. intrepid

# Puzzle 8

Complete the following puzzle using the words you just learned in this chapter. Puzzle solutions are in the back of the book.

## Across

3. produce
6. condemn
9. disorder
10. success
12. fearless
13. conceited
14. guilty

15. submissive
18. comfort
19. to free from

## Down

1. by chance
2. a leader
3. male and female characteristics
4. superficial knowledge
5. oaf
7. soothe
8. upstart
11. affluent person
16. admire
17. destroy

# Crossword Puzzles Answer Key

## Puzzle 1

**Across**

8. transmute

11. trite

14. novice

15. malinger

16. fugitive

18. querulous

20. anarchy

**Down**

1. conundrum

2. unkempt

3. truant

4. volatile

5. reputable

6. perceptive

7. meticulous

9. absolve

10. tedium

12. pariah

13. demure

17. fallacy

19. emend

## Puzzle 2

**Across**

3. criterion

5. raconteur

8. bereft

13. divulge

14. acrimonious

15. cohesive

16. abridge

17. debunk

**Down**

1. camaraderie

2. ostracize

3. cloying

4. audacious

6. obdurate

7. penurious

9. carping

10. egoism

11. spurious

12. depose

13. destitute

18. nadir

# Puzzle 3

## Across

7. aesthetic

8. remorse

9. promulgate

11. quell

13. plenary

15. detractor

16. quotidian

17. frenetic

19. secrete

## Down

1. devious

2. quandary

3. pundit

4. discrepancy

5. corrosive

6. phlegmatic

10. alleviate

12. perdition

13. purify

14. exuberance

18. impeccable

# Puzzle 4

## Across

2. refurbish

6. sustain

7. lucid

8. anomaly

10. expedite

11. feral

12. durable

16. indistinct

18. vestige

19. sagacious

20. relevance

## Down

1. auspicious

3. exculpate

4. expropriate

5. unparalleled

9. repudiate

13. nocturnal

14. digress

15. untenable

17. suppress

# Puzzle 5

**Across**

3. pompous
5. diatribe
6. rife
7. concise
8. jargon
9. pall
10. genial
13. acme
14. covet
16. coup
17. irate
18. cant

**Down**

1. wary
2. sage
3. preamble
4. profane
5. dreg
11. innate
12. neurotic
15. opulent

# Puzzle 6

**Across**

7. ineluctable
9. theology
11. ukase
12. enmity
14. placate
16. obscure
17. discern
18. utopia
19. obtrusive

**Down**

1. jeopardize
2. surreptitious
3. officious
4. onerous
5. mundane
6. oblivious
8. froward
9. tentative
10. revere
13. alienate
15. caducity

## Puzzle 7

**Across**

2. miasma
4. lissome
7. decimate
11. permeate
16. tenebrous
17. inamorata
19. pallid
20. tryst

**Down**

1. osculate
3. nondescript
5. eminent
6. coalesce
8. esculent
9. nomad
10. languid
12. sloth

13. castigate
14. penitent
15. encroach
18. titular

## Puzzle 8

**Across**

3. engender
6. decry
9. chaos
10. éclat
12. intrepid
13. bumptious
14. culpable
15. servile
18. solace

19. extricate

**Down**

1. fluke
2. bellwether
3. epicene
4. sciolism
5. galoot
7. mollify
8. arriviste
11. nabob
16. venerate

17. eradicate

*Get Wise! Mastering Vocabulary Skills*

# appendix
## Word Parts

This list contains some of the common prefixes, roots, and suffixes that make up the building blocks of numerous English words. You should read through this list carefully and come back to it every now and then to jumpstart your memory. We sure don't expect you to sit down and memorize them, but you should work at trying to figure out the meanings of these word parts when you see them in vocabulary words.

## Prefixes

| | | |
|---|---|---|
| **ana-** | up, again, anew, throughout | *analyze*—loosen up, break up into parts |
| | | *anagram*—word spelled by mixing up letters of another word |

| | | |
|---|---|---|
| **ante-** | before | *antediluvian*—before the Flood |
| **anti-** | against | *antiwar*—against war |
| **arch-** | first, chief | *archetype*—first model |
| **auto-** | self | *automobile*—self-moving vehicle |
| **bene-, ben-** | good, well | *benefactor*—one who does good deeds |
| **bi-** | two | *bilateral*—two-sided |
| **circum-** | around | *circumnavigate*—sail around |
| **com-, co-, col-, con-, cor-** | with, together | *concentrate*—bring closer together *cooperate*—work with *collapse*—fall together |
| **contra-, contro-, counter-** | against | *contradict*—speak against *counterclockwise*—against the clock |
| **de-** | away from, down, opposite of | *detract*—draw away from |
| **demi-** | half | *demitasse*—half cup |
| **di-** | twice, double | *dichromatic*—having two colors |
| **dia-** | across, through | *diameter*—measurement across |
| **dis-, di-** | not, away from | *dislike*—to not like *digress*—turn away from the subject |
| **dys-** | bad, poor | *dyslexia*—poor reading |
| **equi-** | equal | *equivalent*—of equal value |
| **ex-, e-, ef-** | from, out | *expatriate*—one who lives outside his or her native country *emit*—send out |

| | | |
|---|---|---|
| **extra-** | outside, beyond | *extraterrestrial*—from beyond Earth |
| **fore-** | in front of, previous | *forecast*—tell ahead of time |
| | | *foreleg*—front leg |
| **geo-** | earth | *geography*—science of the earth's surface |
| **homo-** | same, like | *homophonic*—sounding the same |
| **hyper-** | too much, over | *hyperactive*—overly active |
| **hypo-** | too little, under | *hypothermia*—state of having too little body heat |
| **in-, il-, ig-, im-, ir-** | not | *innocent*—not guilty *ignorant*—not knowing |
| | | *illogical*—not logical |
| | | *irresponsible*—not responsible |
| **in-, il-, im-, ir-** | on, into, in | *impose*—place on |
| | | *invade*—go into |
| **intra-, intro-** | within, inside | *intrastate*—within a state |
| **inter-** | between, among | *interplanetary*—between planets |
| **mal-, male-** | bad, wrong, poor | *maladjust*—adjust poorly |
| | | *malevolent*—ill-wishing |
| **mis-** | badly, wrongly | *misunderstand*—understand wrongly |
| **mis-, miso-** | hatred | *misogyny*—hatred of women |
| **mono-** | single, one | *monorail*—train that runs on a single rail |
| **neo-** | new | *neolithic*—of the New Stone Age |

| | | |
|---|---|---|
| **non-** | not | *nonentity*—a person of thing of little or no importance |
| **ob-** | over, against, toward | *obstruct*—stand against |
| **omni-** | all | *omnipresent*—present in all places |
| **pan-** | all | *panorama*—a complete view |
| **peri-** | around, near | *periscope*—device for seeing all around |
| **poly-** | many | *polygonal*—many-sided |
| **post-** | after | *postmortem*—after death |
| **pre-** | before, earlier than | *prejudice*—judgment in advance |
| **pro-** | in favor of, forward, in front of | *proceed*—go forward<br>*prowar*—in favor of war |
| **re-** | back, again | *rethink*—think again<br>*reimburse*—pay back |
| **retro-** | backward | *retrospective*—looking backward |
| **se-** | apart, away | *seclude*—keep away |
| **semi-** | half | *semiconscious*—half conscious |

Oh, no, I think I'm **semiconscious**—Quick, wake me up!

| | | |
|---|---|---|
| **sub-, suc-, suf-, sug, sus-** | under, beneath | *subscribe*—write underneath<br>*suspend*—hang down<br>*suffer*—undergo |

| | | |
|---|---|---|
| **super-** | above, greater | *superfluous*—overflowing, beyond what is needed |
| **syn-, sym-, syl-, sys-** | with, at the same time | *synthesis*—a putting together |
| | | *sympathy*—a feeling with |
| **tele-** | far | *television*—machine for seeing far |
| **trans-** | across | *transport*—carry across a distance |
| **un-** | not | *uninformed*—not informed |
| **vice-** | acting for, next in rank to | *viceroy*—one acting for the king |

# Roots

| | | |
|---|---|---|
| **alter, altr** | other, change | *alternative, altercation, altruism* |
| **am, amic** | love, friend | *amorous, amiable* |
| **anim** | mind, life, spirit | *animism, animate, animosity* |
| **annu, enni** | year | *annual, superannuated, biennial* |
| **anthrop** | man | *anthropoid, misanthropy* |
| **apt, ept** | fit | *apt, adapt, ineptitude* |
| **aqu** | water | *aquatic, aquamarine* |
| **arbit** | judge | *arbiter, arbitrary* |
| **arch** | chief | *anarchy, matriarch* |
| **arm** | arm, weapon | *army, armature, disarm* |
| **art** | skill, a fitting | *artisan, artifact, articulate* together |
| **aster, astr** | star | *asteroid, disaster, astral* |
| **aud, audit, aur** | hear | *auditorium, audition, auricle* |

| aur | gold | *aureate, aureomycin* |
|---|---|---|
| aut | self | *autism, autograph* |
| bell | war | *antebellum, belligerent* |
| ben, bene | well, good | *benevolent, benefit* |
| bibli | book | *bibliography, bibliophile* |
| bio | life | *biosphere, amphibious* |
| brev | short | *brevity, abbreviation* |
| cad, cas, cid | fall | *cadence, casualty, occasion, accident* |
| cand | white, shining | *candid, candle, incandescent* |
| cant, chant | sing, charm | *cantor, recant, enchant* |
| cap, capt, cept, cip | take, seize, hold | *capable, captive, accept, incipient* |
| capit | head | *capital, decapitate, recapitulate* |
| carn | flesh | *carnal, incarnate* |
| cede, ceed, cess | go, yield | *secede, exceed, process* |
| cent | hundred | *percentage, centimeter* |
| cern, cert | perceive, make certain | *concern, certificate, certain* |
| chrom | color | *monochrome, chromatic* |
| chron | time | *chronometer, anachronism* |
| cide, cis | cut, kill | *genocide, incision* |
| cit | summon, impel | *cite, excite, incitement* |
| civ | citizen | *uncivil, civilization* |
| clam, claim | shout | *clamorous, proclaim, claimant* |
| clar | clear | *clarity, clarion, declare* |

| | | |
|---|---|---|
| **clin** | slope, lean | *inclination, recline* |
| **clud, clus, clos** | close, shut | *seclude, recluse, closet* |
| **cogn** | know | *recognize, incognito* |
| **col, cul** | till | *colony, cultivate, agriculture* |
| **corp** | body | *incorporate, corpse* |
| **cosm** | order, world | *cosmetic, cosmos, cosmopolitan* |
| **crac, crat** | power, rule | *democrat, theocracy* |
| **cre, cresc, cret** | grow | *increase, crescent, accretion* |
| **cred** | trust, believe | *credit, incredible* |
| **crux, cruc** | cross | *crux, crucial, crucifix* |
| **crypt** | hidden | *cryptic, cryptography* |
| **culp** | blame | *culprit, culpability* |
| **cur, curr, curs** | run, course | *occur, current, incursion* |
| **cura** | care | *curator, accurate* |
| **cycl** | wheel, circle | *bicycle, cyclone* |
| **dec** | ten | *decade, decimal* |
| **dem** | people | *demographic, demagogue* |
| **dent** | tooth | *dental, indentation* |
| **derm** | skin | *dermatitis, pachyderm* |
| **di, dia** | day | *diary, quotidian* |
| **dic, dict** | say, speak | *indicative, edict, dictation* |
| **dign** | worthy | *dignified, dignitary* |
| **doc, doct** | teach, prove | *indoctrinate, docile, doctor* |
| **domin** | rule | *predominate, domineer, dominion* |

| | | |
|---|---|---|
| **dorm** | sleep | *dormitory, dormant* |

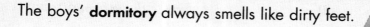

The boys' **dormitory** always smells like dirty feet.

| | | |
|---|---|---|
| **du** | two | *duo, duplicity, dual* |
| **duc, duct** | lead | *educate, abduct, ductile* |
| **dur** | hard, lasting | *endure, obdurate, duration* |
| **dyn** | force, power | *dynamo, dynamite* |
| **ego** | I | *egomania, egotist* |
| **equ** | equal | *equation, equitable* |
| **erg, urg** | work, power | *energetic, metallurgy* |
| **err** | wander | *error, aberrant* |
| **ev** | time, age | *coeval, longevity* |
| **fac, fact, fect, fic** | do, make | *facility, factual, perfect, artifice* |
| **fer** | bear, carry | *prefer, refer, conifer, fertility* |
| **ferv** | boil | *fervid, effervesce* |
| **fid** | belief, faith | *infidelity, confidant, perfidious* |
| **fin** | end, limit | *finite, confine* |
| **firm** | strong | *reaffirm, infirmity* |
| **flect, flex** | bend | *reflex, inflection* |
| **flor** | flower | *florescent, floral* |
| **flu, fluct, flux** | flow | *fluid, fluctuation, influx* |
| **form** | shape | *formative, reform, formation* |
| **fort** | strong | *effort, fortitude* |

| | | |
|---|---|---|
| **frag, fract** | break | *fragility, infraction* |
| **fug** | flee | *refuge, fugitive* |
| **fus** | pour, join | *infuse, transfusion* |
| **gam** | marry | *exogamy, polygamous* |
| **ge, geo** | earth | *geology, geode, perigee* |
| **gen** | birth, kind, race | *engender, general, generation* |
| **gest** | carry, bear | *gestation, ingest, digest* |
| **gon** | angle | *hexagonal, trigonometry* |
| **grad, gress** | step, go | *regress, gradation* |
| **gram** | writing | *grammar, cryptogram* |
| **graph** | writing | *telegraph, graphics* |
| **grat** | pleasing, agreeable | *congratulate, gratuitous* |
| **grav** | weight, heavy | *gravity* |
| **greg** | flock, crowd | *gregarious, segregate* |
| **habit, hibit** | have, hold | *habitation, inhibit, habitual* |
| **heli** | sun | *helium, heliocentric, aphelion* |
| **hem** | blood | *hemoglobin, hemorrhage* |
| **her, hes** | stick, cling | *adherent, cohesive* |
| **hydr** | water | *dehydration, hydrofoil* |
| **iatr** | heal, cure | *pediatrics, psychiatry* |
| **iso** | same, equal | *isotope, isometric* |
| **it** | journey, go | *itinerary, exit* |

My **itinerary** today is to move out and onward to page 210.

| | | |
|---|---|---|
| **ject** | throw | *reject, subjective, projection* |
| **jud** | judge | *judicial, adjudicate* |
| **jug, junct** | join | *conjugal, juncture, conjunction* |
| **jur** | swear | *perjure, jurisprudence* |
| **labor** | work | *laborious, belabor* |
| **leg** | law | *legal, illegitimate* |
| **leg, lig, lect** | choose, gather, read | *illegible, eligible, select, lecture* |
| **lev** | light, rise | *levity, alleviate* |
| **liber** | free | *liberal, libertine* |
| **liter** | letter | *literate, alliterative* |
| **lith** | rock, stone | *neolithic, lithograph* |
| **loc** | place | *locale, locus, allocate* |
| **log** | word, study | *logic, biology, dialogue* |
| **loqu, locut** | talk, speech | *colloquial, loquacious, interlocutor* |
| **luc, lum** | light | *translucent, pellucid, illumine, luminous* |
| **lud, lus** | play | *allusion, ludicrous, interlude* |
| **magn** | large, great | *magnificent, magnitude* |
| **mal** | bad, ill | *malodorous, malinger* |
| **man, manu** | hand | *manifest, manicure, manuscript* |
| **mar** | sea | *maritime, submarine* |
| **mater, matr** | mother | *matriarchal, maternal* |
| **medi** | middle | *intermediary, medieval* |
| **mega** | large, million | *megaphone, megacycle* |
| **ment** | mind | *demented, mental* |

*Get Wise! Mastering Vocabulary Skills*

| merg, mers | plunge, dip | *emerge, submersion* |
|---|---|---|
| meter, metr, mens | measure | *chronometer, metronome, geometry, commensurate* |
| micr | small | *microfilm, micron* |
| min | little | *minimum, minute* |
| mit, miss | send | *remit, admission, missive* |
| mon, monit | warn | *admonish, monument, monitor* |
| mor | custom | *mores, immoral* |
| mor, mort | death | *mortify, mortician* |
| morph | shape | *amorphous, anthropomorphic* |
| mov, mob, mot | move | *removal, automobile, motility* |
| multi | many | *multiply, multinational* |
| mut | change | *mutable, transmute* |
| nasc, nat | born | *native, natural, nascent, innate* |
| nav | ship, sail | *navy, navigable* |
| necr | dead, die | *necropolis, necrosis* |
| neg | deny | *renege, negative* |
| neo | new | *neologism, neoclassical* |
| nomen, nomin | name | *nomenclature, cognomen, nominate* |
| nomy | law, rule | *astronomy, antinomy* |
| nov | new | *novice, innovation* |
| ocul | eye | *binocular, oculist* |
| omni | all | *omniscient, omnibus* |
| onym | name | *pseudonym, eponymous* |
| oper | work | *operate, cooperation, inoperable* |

| | | |
|---|---|---|
| **ora** | speak, pray | *oracle, oratory* |
| **orn** | decorate | *adorn, ornate* |
| **orth** | straight, correct | *orthodox, orthopedic* |
| **pan** | all | *panacea, pantheon* |
| **pater, patr** | father | *patriot, paternity* |
| **path, pat, pass** | feel, suffer | *telepathy, patient, compassion, passion* |
| **ped** | child | *pedagogue, pediatrics* |
| **ped, pod** | foot | *pedestrian, impede, tripod* |
| **pel, puls** | drive, push | *impel, propulsion* |
| **pend, pens** | hang | *pendulous, suspense* |
| **pet, peat** | seek | *petition, impetus, repeat* |
| **phil** | love | *philosopher, Anglophile* |
| **phob** | fear | *phobic, agoraphobia* |
| **phon** | sound | *phonograph, symphony* |
| **phor** | bearing | *semaphore, metaphor* |
| **phot** | light | *photograph, photoelectric* |
| **pon, pos** | place, put | *component, repose, postpone* |
| **port** | carry | *report, portable, deportation* |
| **pot** | power | *potency, potential* |
| **press** | press | *pressure, impression* |
| **prim** | first | *primal, primordial* |
| **proto, prot** | first | *proton, protagonist* |
| **psych** | mind | *psychic, metempsychosis* |
| **pyr** | fire | *pyrite, pyrophobia* |

| | | |
|---|---|---|
| **quer, quir, quis, ques** | ask, seek | *query, inquiry, inquisitive, quest* |
| **reg, rig, rect** | straight, rule | *regulate, dirigible, corrective* |
| **rid, ris** | laugh | *deride, risible, ridiculous* |
| **rog** | ask | *rogation, interrogate* |
| **rupt** | break | *erupt, interruption, rupture* |
| **sanct** | holy | *sacrosanct, sanctify, sanction* |
| **sci, scio** | know | *nescient, conscious, omniscience* |
| **scop** | watch, view | *horoscope, telescopic* |
| **scrib, script** | write | *scribble, proscribe, description* |
| **sed, sid, sess** | sit, seat | *sedate, residence, session* |
| **seg, sect** | cut | *segment, section, intersect* |
| **sent, sens** | feel, think | *nonsense, sensitive, sentient, dissent* |
| **sequ, secut** | follow | *sequel, consequence, consecutive* |
| **sign** | sign, mark | *signature, designate, assign* |
| **sol** | alone | *solitary, solo, desolate* |
| **solv, solu, solut** | loosen | *dissolve, soluble, absolution* |
| **somn** | sleep | *insomnia, somnolent* |
| **son** | sound | *sonorous, unison* |
| **soph** | wise, wisdom | *philosophy, sophisticated* |
| **spec, spic, spect** | look | *specimen, conspicuous, spectacle* |
| **spir** | breathe | *spirit, conspire, respiration* |
| **stab, stat** | stand | *unstable, status, station, establish* |
| **stead** | place | *instead, steadfast* |
| **string, strict** | bind | *astringent, stricture, restrict* |
| **stru, struct** | build | *construe, structure, destructive* |

| | | |
|---|---|---|
| **sum, sumpt** | take | *presume, consumer, assumption* |
| **tang, ting, tact, tig** | touch | *tangent, contingency, contact, tactile, contiguous* |
| **tax, tac** | arrange, arrangement | *taxonomy, tactic* |
| **techn** | skill, art | *technique, technician* |
| **tele** | far | *teletype, telekinesis* |
| **tempor** | time | *temporize, extemporaneous* |
| **ten, tain, tent** | hold | *tenant, tenacity, retention, contain* |
| **tend, tens, tent** | stretch | *contend, extensive, intent* |
| **tenu** | thin | *tenuous, attenuate* |
| **term** | end | *terminal, terminate* |
| **terr, ter** | land, earth | *inter, terrain* |
| **test** | witness | *attest, testify* |
| **the** | god | *polytheism, theologist* |
| **therm** | heat | *Thermos, isotherm* |
| **tom** | cut | *atomic, appendectomy* |
| **tort, tors** | twist | *tortuous, torsion, contort* |
| **tract** | pull, draw | *traction, attract, protract* |
| **trib** | assign, pay | *attribute, tribute, retribution* |
| **trud, trus** | thrust | *obtrude, intrusive* |
| **turb** | agitate | *perturb, turbulent, disturb* |
| **umbr** | shade | *umbrella, penumbra, umbrage* |
| **uni** | one | *unify, disunity, union* |
| **urb** | city | *urbane, suburb* |
| **vac** | empty | *vacuous, evacuation* |

| | | |
|---|---|---|
| **vad, vas** | go | *invade, evasive* |
| **val, vail** | strength, worth | *valid, avail, prevalent* |
| **ven, vent** | come | *advent, convene, prevention* |
| **ver** | true | *aver, veracity, verity* |
| **verb** | word | *verbose, adverb, verbatim* |
| **vert, vers** | turn | *revert, perversion* |
| **vest** | dress | *vestment* |
| **vid, vis** | see | *video, evidence, vision, revise* |
| **vinc, vict** | conquer | *evince, convict, victim* |
| **viv, vit** | life | *vivid, revive, vital* |
| **voc, vok** | call | *vociferous, provocative, revoke* |
| **vol** | wish | *involuntary, volition* |
| **voly, volut** | roll, turn | *involve, convoluted, revolution* |
| **vulg** | common | *divulge, vulgarity* |
| **zo** | animal | *zoologist, paleozoic* |

# Suffixes

| | | |
|---|---|---|
| **-cy** | act, state, or position of | *presidency*—position of president *ascendancy*—state of being raised up |
| **-dom** | state, rank, that which belongs to | *wisdom*—state of being wise |
| **-ence** | act, state, or quality of | *dependence*—state of depending |
| **-er, -or** | one who, that | *doer*—one who does which *conductor*—that which conducts |

| | | |
|---|---|---|
| **-escent** | becoming | *obsolescent*—becoming obsolete |
| **-fy** | to make | *pacify*—make peaceful |
| **-hood** | state, condition | *adulthood*—state of being adult |
| **-ic, -ac** | of, like | *demonic*—of or like a demon |
| **-il, -ile** | having to do with, like, suitable for | *civil*—having to do with citizens<br>*tactile*—having to do with touch |
| **-ion** | act or condition of | *operation*—act of operating |
| **-ious** | having, characterized by | *anxious*—characterized by anxiety |
| **-ish** | like, somewhat | *foolish*—like a fool |
| **-ism** | belief or practice | *racism*—belief in racial of superiority |
| **-ist** | one who does, makes, or is | *scientist*—one concerned with science |
| **-ity, -ty, -y** | character or state | *amity*—friendship of being<br>*jealousy*—state of being jealous |
| **-ive** | of, relating to, tending to | *destructive*—tending to destroy |
| **-logue, -loquy** | speech or writing | *monologue*—speech by one person<br>*colloquy*—conversation |

My English teacher's **monologue** was so boring that it almost put me to sleep.

| | | |
|---|---|---|
| **-logy** | speech, study of | *geology*—study of the earth |
| **-ment** | act or state of | *abandonment*—act of abandoning |
| **-mony** | a resulting thing, condition, or state | *patrimony*—property inherited from one's father |
| **-ness** | act or quality | *kindness*—quality of being kind |
| **-ory** | having the quality of; a place or thing for | *compensatory*—having the quality of a compensation<br>*lavatory*—place for washing |
| **-ous, -ose** | full of, having | *glamorous*—full of glamour |
| **-ship** | skill, state of being | *horsemanship*—skill in riding<br><br>*ownership*—state of being an owner |
| **-some** | full of, like | *frolicsome*—playful |
| **-tude** | state or quality of | *rectitude*—state of being morally upright |
| **-ward** | in the direction of | *homeward*—in the direction of home |
| **-y** | full of, like, somewhat | *wily*—full of wiles |